crime and human rights
criminology of genocide and atrocities

Joachim J. Savelsberg

Los Angeles | London | New Delhi
Singapore | Washington DC

SAGE Publications Ltd
1 Oliver's Yard
55 City Road
London EC1Y 1SP

SAGE Publications Inc.
2455 Teller Road
Thousand Oaks, California 91320

SAGE Publications India Pvt Ltd
B 1/I 1 Mohan Cooperative Industrial Area
Mathura Road, New Delhi 110 044
India

SAGE Publications Asia-Pacific Pte Ltd
33 Pekin Street #02-01
Far East Square
Singapore 048763

Library of Congress Control Number 2009933602

British Library Cataloguing in Publication data

A catalogue record for this book is available from the British Library

ISBN 978-1-84787-924-0 (hbk)
ISBN 978-1-84787-925-7 (pbk)

Typeset by C&M Digitals (P) Ltd, Chennai, India
Printed by CPI Antony Rowe, Chippenham, Wiltshire
Printed on paper from sustainable resources

For Anna and Rebecca

contents

acknowledgements

A number of people and institutions contributed to this project; Liz Boyle, Amelia Corl, David Garland, John Hagan, Nicole Rafter, Paul Rock, Jim Short, Kathryn Sikkink, Simon Singer, and Philip Smith read and commented on an early draft of the manuscript; anonymous reviewers provided helpful feedback on the proposal. While I may not have done justice to all suggestions and critiques, they did help improve the text. At the University of Minnesota, the College of Liberal Arts granted a fall 2007 Fellowship at its Institute for Advanced Study and a fall 2008 Single Semester Leave. This book would not have been written without the initiative of Nicole Rafter and Paul Rock. Finally, the professionalism of Caroline Porter at Sage is always appreciated. Thanks to all!

As usual, my wife Pamela Feldman-Savelsberg, anthropologist, Africanist and companion of a quarter century supported me. The cultural trauma of atrocities and the hope for a more respectful and peaceful coexistence helped bring, and hold, us together. We hope that Anna and Rebecca will be part of our contribution. To them this book is dedicated.

Joachim J. Savelsberg
Minneapolis/Saint Paul, 2009

introduction:
how have governments responded to atrocities and human rights violations?

After a brief introduction about this book, and me the author, there follows a description of selected atrocities, grave violations of human rights (HR) and humanitarian law (HL) from which we gain insights into the variations and commonalities of offenses and responses.

The emergence of HR law and the criminalization of atrocities is one of the most important developments in recent criminology and penal law. Yet most scholars who study crimes against humanity, war crimes, and genocide, primarily historians, political scientists, and legal scholars, make no use of criminological insights. Simultaneously, innovative criminologists have only recently begun to address HR and HL violations. Their contribution is crucial as such violations, during the twentieth century alone cost the lives of almost two hundred million people, and resulted in hundreds of millions of cases of rape, torture, looting, arson and displacement—a toll that far outnumbers victimizations through street crimes. This book advances a sociologically based criminology of humanitarian and HR crimes and their control. Both HR scholars and criminologists should benefit, as should the institutions that may contribute to civilizing the behavior of political and military leaders and their front-line agents.

Human rights are those political, legal, social and economic rights that are granted to all humans, independent of their citizenship, through common law and international conventions. They include the right to free speech, religion and fair trials, and protection from torture and genocide. The idea of HR is historically new, dating back to the Enlightenment era, and institutional responses against violations, especially their criminalization, are most recent, dating to the post-World War II era. HR trail the slightly earlier emergence of HL, codified by the Geneva and Hague Conventions that seek to protect non-combatants against atrocities in times of warfare. Both HL and HR law begin to restrict the older notion of state sovereignty under which states could act toward their citizens at will, without the risk of interference by the international community. Both are addressed in this volume, while the focus is on the gravest of violations.

Throughout this book, I seek a conversation with you, the reader, by raising a series of questions, marked by the chapter titles. The chapters provide answers, but they also leave room for discussion. After sketching, in this introduction, atrocities and control responses across time and space, Part I explores historical variation. Why is it, as Harvard law professor Martha Minow (2002) finds, that the twentieth century may have many competitors when it comes to excessive cruelties, but is the first century that gets serious about developing control responses? When and how did atrocities become defined as crimes (Chapter 1), and what types of control responses emerged (Chapter 2)? Part II takes a closer look at the conditions of offending behavior, specifically for the case of genocide and with a focus on the Holocaust. It asks what concepts and explanations criminology can contribute and what it can learn from other fields (Chapters 3 and 4). Chapter 5 provides examples for directions criminology might take to address more recent and contemporary atrocities (My Lai) and genocides (Darfur). Part III asks if and how HR violations can be fought. What new types of criminal courts emerged, and under what conditions do they work (Chapter 6)? Finally, how effective can criminal proceedings be, through deterrence and the cultivation of collective memories of evil, and how do they relate to other control institutions such as quasi-traditional courts or truth commissions (Chapter 7)?

As for the author, with whom you will engage in this conversation, I am a professor of sociology, specializing in criminology and the sociology of law at the University of Minnesota. I was born in 1951, raised and educated in (West) Germany, entering this world just six years after my home country had executed the Holocaust, the most meticulously planned and one of the most deadly genocides in human history. I grew up in a world in which that history was silenced, and my generation began to awake to its terrible truths only in the course of the late 1960s. Our country's history of totalitarianism, war of aggression, war crimes and genocide has been a permanent companion ever since. We learned to live in the shadow of its history and sought to live up to the resulting responsibility. One way for a scholar to do so, is through engagement in research about the conditions of atrocities and about mechanisms of response and prevention. We shall see throughout the text that members of many societies have plentiful reason to join into the effort. Strict adherence to the principle of national sovereignty is no longer acceptable, and institutions must be considered through which the international community can effectively intervene.

What shape do atrocities take and what responses do they encounter?

On a summer day in mid-July 1995, with civil war raging in the Balkan republic of Bosnia, a young soldier named Dražen Erdemović unexpectedly found himself as a member of an eight-man execution squad. During a six hour shift he and his companions shot some 1,200 unarmed civilian men, before another squad took over the exhausting work. The killings took place near the town of Srebrenica. They were part of a huge and murderous ethnic cleansing action conducted by a contingent of the Bosnian-Serb army against Bosnian Muslims. In the preceding days Muslim men of military age had been separated from women and children. The latter were bused away, while more than 7,000 men were killed in four nearby execution sites and buried in five mass graves. Once growing international attention began to worry the perpetrators, they set heavy equipment in motion to conceal their atrocity, advancing reburials to 30 different, more distant and smaller sites. The military action was overseen by Major-General Radislav Krstić, a career soldier and self-described family man, himself under orders by General Ratko Mladic, leader of the Bosnian-Serb military. The execution campaign by Mr. Erdemović and his comrades under the leadership of their generals was to have judicial consequences at the International Criminal Tribunal for the former Yugoslavia (ICTY), the ad hoc court set up by the United Nations in 1992 in the Dutch capital of The Hague. Erdemović, perpetrator-turned witness, was convicted and sentenced to a ten-year prison term in 1996, a penalty that was later reduced to five years, partly due to the remorse he expressed and his cooperation with the Tribunal. In March 2000 a trial began against former General Krstić, captured on 2 December 1998 by American troops. Fifty-five days of testimony, 1,000 exhibits, including photos of mass graves from the air, the ground and from below ground level, depicting some 2,000 exhumed victims, documents and intercepts providing information about the command structure within the units involved in the massacre, and 60 witnesses reflected the massive investigatory and judicial effort that went into this case. On 3 August 2001, Major-General Krstić was convicted for his role in the worst massacre committed in Europe since the Holocaust and sentenced to 46 years in prison (see Hagan 2003: 174).

The Srebrenica massacre was, of course, only one of many actions in a series of murderous wars that engulfed the former Yugoslavia in the 1990s. In the end more than 200,000 were killed; the number of often unimaginably brutal rapes—many committed in "rape houses"— can only be roughly estimated at 20,000 to 50,000; and more than two million were displaced. Much of this activity was supported by the former Serb and Yugoslav president, Slobodan Milošević, who was himself tried before the ICTY, but who died on 6 March 2006, shortly before a verdict could be reached.

While the murder machine in the Balkans was raging, some thousand miles to the South, in the Republic of South Africa, the infamous apartheid regime was coming to an end. It had endured for over almost a half a century from 1948 to 1994, maintained its radical separation of racial groups, the economic and legal deprivation of Black and "colored" Africans, with brute force against all who sought to resist it. The system of repression during South Africa's apartheid involved many actors, from top government leaders down to the executors of dirty work. Consider Jeffrey Benzien, a police officer who had joined the South African force in 1977, became a detective and was soon moved into a murder-and-robbery squad, known for torturing criminals. Mr. Benzien lived an unobtrusive life in his Cape Town suburban home from which he went to work every morning to return home for dinner with his wife and children. Almost a decade after joining the force he was selected for the more prestigious security branch, charged with the investigation of political activists. Here torture was pervasive. Victims accused him of beatings, of being hung for hours by handcuffs, and having a broomstick shoved up their rectums; but officer Benzien's speciality was the "wet bag" method of placing a soaked cloth over the victims' heads, taking them close to asphyxiation, and doing so repeatedly. Questioned by Peter Jacobs, one of his victims in later hearings before the Truth and Reconciliation Commission, about the torture methods he had exposed him to, he answered: "If I say to Mr. Jacobs I put the electrodes on his nose I may be wrong … If I say I attached them to his genitals, I may be wrong. If I say I put a probe in his rectum, I may be wrong. I could have used any one of those methods" (quoted after Daley in Ermann and Lundman 2002: 189).

Officer Benzien of course was just one of many wheels in a large machinery of apartheid brutality. His actions, like those of Mr. Erdemović and Mr. Krstić provoked institutional responses. Yet, the institution was not a criminal court, but the South African Truth and Reconciliation Commission (TRC). In February of 1999 the TRC granted Mr. Benzien amnesty. The decision was based on the commission's understanding that the former police officer's actions had been politically motivated and that he had confessed everything. It was also understood that he had followed explicit and implicit orders. But again, Officer Brenzien did not act alone. Only in tandem with thousands of perpetrators at various levels of government hierarchy could tens of thousands be killed, tortured and forced into emigration during South Africa's apartheid regime.

From South Africa we move across the Atlantic Ocean to Latin America. A victim of the Argentinean "Dirty War," conducted by a series of military juntas against opponents of the regime between 1976 and 1984, remembers:

At 4 a.m. on 21 April 1976, several men in civilian clothes forced their way into my house. They were heavily armed and identified themselves as belonging to the Navy and the Federal Police. Their commander said he was Inspector Mayorga. They took away my father, who was sixty-five at that time. The following day my brother Miguel presented a writ of habeas corpus at the San Isidro court. At 9 p.m. on that same day they came back to my house, this time taking away my mother, hooded. They took her somewhere she has never been able to identify, and for five days subjected her to a violent interrogation. Following her capture, the members of the Armed Forces stayed on in my house. On April 23

> my brother Miguel was kidnapped as he entered ... My mother was set
> free, blindfolded, two blocks from our house. My father and brother have
> never reappeared ... (Nunca Mas 1986: 16).

Most perpetrators in this and thousands of other instances of abduction,
torture and killing remain unnamed. They acted under a brutal dictatorship that came to power through a military coup on 23–24 March 1976,
welcomed by many Argentineans after several years of terrorist violence
from both the extreme left and right. Referring to the police and military
under a three-man junta, led by Lt. General Jorge Rafael Videla (later
Generals Roberto Viola and Leopolodo Fortunato Galtieri), the Argentinean Truth Commission concluded:

> By far the most common method they adopted, as this report sadly
> details, was simply to make a person 'disappear,' That is, someone would
> be captured by (usually anonymous) members of the security forces, from
> which moment on there would be a systematic denial from all levels of
> the state security or legal bodies of any knowledge about them ... The great
> majority of these unfortunate people who had disappeared were then
> deliberately killed, often after being subjected to prolonged torture ...
> (Nunca Mas 1986: xiv).

During the most intense period between 1976 and 1978 between 9,800
and 20,000 people are estimated to have disappeared and were never
seen again. Economic policy failures and hardship, combined with
military defeat in the June 1982 Falkland War against the British armed
forces, resulted in a thorough delegitimization of the military regime.
The final military president, Reynaldo Bignone, then led the country to
renewed free elections. He also, however, declared an amnesty for all
involved in the Junta's "Dirty War." Yet, on 10 December 1983, Raúl
Alfonsín, the first freely elected president after the military dictatorship, established the National Commission on Disappeared People
(CONADEP), a truth commission that delivered the comprehensive
report from which I cited above on 20 September 1984, entitled Nunca
Mas (www.nuncamas.org). Partly based on evidence gained by the commission, the nine leaders of the three military juntas were tried by a
civilian criminal court. On 9 December 1985 the court announced that
five of the nine commanders-in-chief were criminally liable. Sentences

ranged from four and a half years to life imprisonment with absolute disqualification from holding public office. Alfonsín's Peronist successor, Carlos Menem, however, pardoned those convicted in December 1990. One year earlier he had declared a quasi-amnesty aborting trials against almost 400 defendants of lower rank (Punto Final and Due Obedience laws), with considerable public support but against serious constitutional concerns.

Also on other continents, the history of HR and HL offenses is long. Consider North America with the near-extermination of Native Americans during the colonial period and after the foundation of the United States, or First Nations peoples in Canada, the history of slave trade and slavery, Jim Crow laws and lynching campaigns, with frequent cooperation by local law enforcement. Also wars fought by the United States were accompanied by grave offenses against HL and HR law. Debate still rages over the massive bombardment of civilian targets (or the lack of bombardment of train tracks leading into the extermination camps of the Nazis) during World War II. Among massacres of civilian populations, the most infamous is that of hundreds committed in the village of My Lai during the Vietnam War. After one year of denial by the military, the event attracted broad attention through the Pulitzer Price winning book by journalist Seymour Hersh (1970) and an Army Commission Report drafted under General Peers (Goldstein et al. 1976). We will explore this incident in Chapter 5. More recently torture and abuses of prisoners in occupied countries have become known, most infamously through the Abu Ghraib prison scandal in Iraq. Responses to these crimes differ from reactions described above for the Balkan, apartheid and Argentinean cases. In the My Lai case, for example, where the Peers commission had documented wrongdoing on the part of at least 30 participants up to the level of generality, charges were filed against 12, four of which went to trial. The final result was the conviction and punishment of one relatively low-level defendant (Lt. Calley), whose sentence to life imprisonment was reduced, through executive intervention, first to 20 and later to 10 years, but who was released after three years.

Not all violations of HL and HR law involve torture and mass killings. Comparatively minor types of offenses include police brutality such as the infamous 1992 brutal beating of Rodney King, an African-American motorist, by officers of the Los Angeles police department; forced evictions of Sinti and Roma from their homes reported in recent years especially from Central-Eastern European countries and Italy; the overcrowding of jail cells in countries like Brazil, where inmates may have to take turns to lay down for sleep; solitary confinement in extremely artificial environments where lights are never turned off in American high security prisons; mass arrests of political opponents and activists in the PRC or in Burma. Such HR violations demand political and scholarly attention; and criminology has tools with which to address these behaviors. Yet, in this volume we will focus on those gravest of violations that typically involve massive loss of human lives such as crimes against humanity, genocide and war crimes.

Devastating as cases such as Srebrenica and My Lai are to those affected, and shocking to those who care to look, they are still only minor instances compared to the major atrocities committed by governments and their agents at all levels of hierarchy against their own subjects and citizens of other countries throughout history. Political scientist R.J. Rummel assembled one of the most comprehensive summaries of *Death by Government* with a massive collection of data on government-induced democides committed during the twentieth century through 1987. By democide, Rummel (1994: 31) means "the murder of any person or people by a government, including genocide, politicide [the murder of groups because of their politics or for political purposes], and mass murder [indiscriminate killing]."

The numbers are staggering, and they are worth noting—even if some are only rough estimates and others may be debated. Rummel (1994: 4) lists "Dekamegamurderers," those who killed in the tens of millions, including the USSR, from 1917–87, the PRC from 1949–87, Germany from 1933–1945, and nationalist China (KMT) from 1928–49. Their death toll adds up to more than 128 million people. Lesser "Megamurderers" of more than 19 million include Japan (1936–45), Mao's Soviets in China (1923–49), Cambodia (1975–79), Turkey (1909–18), Vietnam (1945–87), Poland (1945–48), Pakistan (1958–87), and Yugoslavia under Tito (1944–87). Most of these killings and numbers are known to students of world history. Given history's sloppy accounting of millions of deaths, however, other Megamurderers are only suspected, including North Korea (1948–87), Mexico (1900–20) and Russia (1900–17), adding another good four million dead to the toll. Finally, "Centi-Kilomurderers", those who killed "only" in the hundreds of thousands, jointly contributed another 15 million or so to the total of 169.202 million individuals murdered by their own or other peoples' governments between 1900 and 1987. And again, this number does not include the hundreds of millions of human lives taken in government-initiated wars.

Consider, by way of comparison, the number of individuals who fell victim to murder, manslaughter and homicide in civil society around the globe. Adding up all victims of these crimes in a year closest to 1970 for which data were available (Archer and Gartner 1984), and rounding up generously, yields some 100,000 victims. Doubling this number to account for countries for which data were unavailable and multiplying the resulting 200,000 victims by the number of years included in Rummel's analysis (87), the total of 1.74 million killed constitutes just about 1 percent of the total number of people murdered by governments. Clearly, if criminologists have anything to contribute to our understanding of violent crime, including crime committed by governments, criminological insights should be brought to bear in this enterprise.

The cases summarized here vary in many ways, including methods of killings, their execution in times of peace versus war, and the number of victims. Yet, there are also commonalities. All involve collective action, with front-line, low-level actors who executed the dirty work as well as leaders whose hands remain untainted by the blood for the shedding of which they bear ultimate responsibility. Many thus constitute *organizational crimes*, understood here as "crimes conducted with the support of an organization whose goals they are intended to advance" (Coleman 2006: 11). These are typically legitimate organizations, corporations or government agencies. Some are cases of *organized crime* when offenses are committed by criminal organizations, set up for the purpose of engaging in law-breaking behavior. Examples are the Mafia or the SA or SS, the German Nazi Party's own armed troops. At times, actors involved in organizational activities, legal or illegal, also seek to satisfy their own greed or sadistic desires—independent of, or even disadvantageous to, the organization's goals. It is thus useful to also consider *occupational crime*, "committed by individuals in the course of their occupation for their personal gain and without organizational support" (Coleman 2006: 11). These distinctions are not always easy to uphold in our context as we will see. But importantly, all of the transgressions introduced so far

Table 1   Selected Atrocities (19th and 20th Centuries) by Government Response[1]

	Response(s)								
Atrocities	1	2	3	4	5	6	7	8	9
Slave trade/Slavery in the United States (–1865)	–	–	–	–	–	–	–	–	–
Slavery in Brazil (–1888)	–	–	–	–	–	–	–	–	–
Forced adoption of Aboriginals, Australia (1900–80s)	–	–	–	–	–	–	–	1992ff	–
Trail of Tears against Cherokees (1838)	–	–	–	–	–	–	–	2000	–
German Genocide against Herero and Mana (1904–07)	–	–	–	–	–	–	–	2004	–
Ottoman Genocide against Armenians (1914–15)	–	–	–	–	–	–	–	–	–
Stalinist Purges (especially 1930s)	–	–	–	–	–	–	–	–	1995
Atrocities in Spanish civil war; Franco repression (1936–39)	2008	–	–	–	–	–	1977	–	–
Nazi-German Holocaust against Jews (1941–45)	1962ff	1945ff	1952ff	–	–	–	1947ff	1970ff	1960ff
Arial bombing of civilian populations, WWII (1943–45)	–	–	–	–	–	–	–	–	–
Japanese atrocities against Chinese (1937ff)	–	1945	–	–	–	–	–	X	–
Anti-Communist atrocities in Korea (1948)	–	–	–	2000	–	–	–	2004	2008
French massacres against Algerians (1955–62)	–	–	–	–	–	–	–	–	2001
South African apartheid (1948–90)	1996ff	–	–	1995–2003	–	–	–	1996	–
Communist repression in Eastern Europe (1948–89)	X	–	–	1992–94	–	1990	–	–	1990
Chinese Culture Revolution (1966–69)	–	–	–	–	–	–	–	–	–
American massacres during Vietnam War (1968)	1970–71	–	–	–	1969–71	–	–	–	–

Table 1 (Continued)

Atrocities	Response(s)								
	1	2	3	4	5	6	7	8	9
Uganda (disappearances under Idi Amin Dada) (1971ff)	–	–	–	1974, 1986–95	–	–	–	–	–
Democide in Cambodia (Pol Pot) (1975–79)	1985	2008	–	–	–	–	–	1999	X
"Dirty War" in Argentina (1976–83)	–	X	–	1983–84	–	–	–	X	2007
Repression and massacres in El Salvador (1980–91)	–	–	–	1992–93	–	–	X	–	–
Chilean repression under General Pinochet (1973–88)	2000	1998	2004	1990–91	–	–	1978	–	–
Repression/massacres in Guatemala (early 1980s–96)	X	2006	1997–99	1998	–	X	–	–	–
Genocide in the Balkans (1992–99)	–	1994–	–	2002–05	–	–	–	X	–
Indonesian genocide in East Timor (1975–99)	–	2000	–	–	–	–	–	2001	–
Repression in Burma/Myanmar (1970s–)	–	–	–	–	–	–	–	–	–
Iraqi genocide against Kurds (1987f)	2006	–	–	–	–	2004	–	–	–
Rwandan genocide against Tutsi (1994)	1996	1995	–	–	–	–	–	–	2004
Democide in Sierra Leone (1991–2003)	–	2002	–	2000–01	–	–	–	–	–
Genocide in Southern Sudan (1980s–)	–	–	–	–	–	–	–	–	–
Genocide in Darfur region of Sudan (2003–)	–	2008ff	–	–	–	–	–	–	–

[1]Atrocities are listed in approximate chronological order. Codes for responses: 1 = domestic court; 2 = other court (e.g., foreign, victors, international, hybrid); 3 = reparations; 4 = truth (and reconciliation) commission; 5 = other commission; 6 = lustration/vetting; 7 = amnesty; 8 = apology; 9 = memorials in perpetrator country; X = applies, but date unspecified.

constitute crimes in a legal sense as many offended against domestic law and all of them were committed after the passing of international HL and HR law—reason enough to place them high on the criminological agenda. Yet, while some of these crimes occurred relatively close to us, most were committed in far away places. Geographic—and social—distance have consequences for cognitive, moral and legal responses to them.

Finally, despite similarities between the crimes outlined above, we also see massive variation in terms of actual legal responses, which American legal thinker and Supreme Court Justice Oliver Wendell Holmes famously called *law in action*. Reactions vary from domestic criminal law to international criminal law, from truth commissions alone to combinations of truth commissions and criminal trials, from courts-martials to public apologies by government officials, possibly combined with reparation payments. Other cases involve vetting (or "lustration"), the banning of categories of people, such as members of the previous ruling party, from government jobs. Yet other cases, including some of the gravest, lack any kind of institutional reaction. In fact, atrocities may be more or less successfully denied, individually and collectively, through factual ("it did not happen"), interpretive ("what happened was really something different") or implicatory ("it happened, but I was not part of it") denial (Cohen 2001). Table 1 gives an overview of the considerable variation in institutional responses to a selection of the many atrocities committed during the past two centuries in chronological order. It also shows that responses become more likely in most recent decades, including delayed responses to older atrocities.

The answer to the guiding question of this introduction is thus clear: Atrocities show great variation, but they also share features. They typically involve collective action and cause immense suffering to many. And, government responses to atrocities also vary greatly. Especially remarkable is a historic trend toward acknowledgement and control responses. This observation leads us to the questions in Part I.

PART I

Are there trends in controlling human rights violations?

To answer this question we first look at human history as a history of atrocities. Simultaneously we examine the conditions under which such atrocities would become considered "crimes" (Chapter 1). We then examine how out of these new conditions grew innovative interventions; a first overview of laws and institutions is provided (Chapter 2).

ONE

when are atrocities crimes?

Sketching human history as a history of atrocities, we see that atrocities were not always considered crimes, modern behavioral definitions and ideas of natural law notwithstanding. Yet, perpetrators of the twentieth century drew false lessons from this history when they believed they could act with impunity. New conditions had taken hold to pave the way for a new understanding of atrocities as crimes.

All human history, at least the history of state-organized societies, is also a history of atrocities, defined here as behaviors, through which government agents or others invited or tolerated by governments, impose immense cruelty upon segments of a population. An examination of numerous world regions throughout history reveals a multitude of institutional mechanisms through which people were gravely mistreated or murdered en masse; including slavery, infanticide, maltreatment and killing of prisoners of war, and colonial exploitation (see Rummel 1994: 45–75 on the following).

Early on, wherever ancient rulers dominated over vast empires, the lives of hundreds of thousands were at risk, especially in periods of conquest. The name of Genghis Khan appears frequently in historic accounts. During his 1219 capture of Bokhara and Samarkand he had tens of thousands of the cities' inhabitants killed. In 1220 he had 50,000 killed in Kazvin and 70,000 in Nessa. In 1221, the capture of the Persian city of Merv was followed by the slaughter of 1.3 million inhabitants during a 13 day-period. When he conquered Jayy, a city with 3,000 mosques, Genghis Khan initially spared the population. Yet, after a rebellion broke out, he had 1.6 million inhabitants killed. His successors clearly sought to fill his shoes. In 1258, following the capture of Baghdad, Khulagu had 800,000 of its inhabitants slaughtered. And, Khubilai Khan, in his wars of conquest against China between 1252 and 1279, had more than 18 million Chinese killed. Altogether more than 30 million Persian, Arab, Hindu, European and Chinese men, women and children were murdered during a half a century alone.

Not all mass killers receive the attention they deserve. We will only mention two famous Sultans of the twelfth and thirteenth centuries, Kutb'd Aibak of Delhi who had his subjects slaughtered by the hundreds of thousands and Ahmed Shah who staged three-day celebrations whenever the number of Hindus killed reached 20,000 per day. Among the Ottoman Sultans, Mohamed II had thousands massacred after the conquest of Constantinople in 1452 and Sultan Abdul Hamid had some 100,000 Armenians killed between 1894 and 1896 (only to be vastly outdone by his successors in government during World War I). Altogether the Sultans of the Ottoman Empire are responsible for the killing of some two million Armenians, Bulgars, Serbs, Greeks and Turks. Across the Atlantic Ocean, enemies of major empires did not fare better. In 1487, the Aztecs had tens of thousands of adversaries ritually killed on one single occasion. A Western observer claims to have counted more than 100,000 skulls on a single rack outside the city walls.

Closer to home for Western readers, mass killings were motivated by religious and revolutionary fervor. The Revolutionary Councils of the French Revolution ordered the execution of some 20,000 members of the nobility, political opponents and alleged traitors. Earlier, the Duke of Alba, acting for the Spanish Crown, had some 18,000 Protestants murdered in the Low Countries between 1567 and 1573. Charles IX of France or his court had tens of thousands of Protestant Huguenots massacred in the infamous St. Bartholomew night of 1572. Yet earlier, in 1099, after the conquest of Jerusalem, Christian Crusaders butchered 40–70,000 of the city's Jewish and Muslim inhabitants.

A few decades later, Archbishop William of Tyre (1943), himself assumed to be of Frankish descent, and the most prominent chronicler of the events of the eleventh century, reports about that fateful 15 July 1099:

It was impossible to look upon the vast numbers of the slain without horror; everywhere lay fragments of human bodies, and the very ground was covered with the blood of the slain. It was not alone the spectacle of headless bodies and mutilated limbs strewn in all directions that roused horror in all who look upon them. Still more dreadful it was to gaze upon the victors themselves, dripping with blood from head to foot, an ominous sight which brought terror to all who met them. It is reported that within the Temple enclosure alone about ten thousand infidels perished ... (p.372).

On one occasion, hundreds of Jews were locked into a synagogue and burned alive, together with their house of worship. Later, during the plagues of the fourteenth century, Christians of the German countries used their Jewish neighbors as scapegoats. In the town of Mainz alone 6,000 Jews were killed. Few Jews were left in Germany after the campaigns had run their course, an outcome similar to that of twentieth century Nazi persecution. Further, the Catholic Church's treatment of heretics is well known: 32,000 were killed by fire, often through slow burning; another 125,000 are estimated to have died from miserable prison conditions and torture between 1480 and 1809. And Protestant witch hunts cost the lives of thousands of women (Jensen 2007).

Slavery, slave trade and colonialism, and their immense cost in human lives, must not be left out. Between the sixteenth and nineteenth centuries, some 1.5 million to 2 million African slaves were killed by the deplorable conditions of their voyage across the ocean. Millions more perished during their transports to the Middle East and the Orient. Rummel (1994: 48) estimates the total death toll at somewhere between 17 and 65 million.

Finally, while some chapters of colonial cruelty are well known, many are forgotten. The 1904–7 German genocide against the Herero in today's Namibia, the first in the twentieth century, cost some 24,000 to 75,000 lives; 50 to 70 percent of the Herero population was murdered (Steinmetz 2007). Mass killings by the British are reported from today's Borneo in 1849. The Dutch colonizers orchestrated massacres of up to 80,000 Chinese in Jakarta (then Batavia) and similar campaigns in Java. In America, the Puritans killed some 500–600 Pequot Indians, the French about 1,000 Nanchez Indians in the lower Mississippi. Some 4,000 Cheyenne died during the infamous "trail of tears," during resettlement via death march, from their native Georgia to areas west of the

Mississippi River under President van Buren. The total population loss is estimated at eight to 110 million. The Native American population was reduced to one tenth of its original size in the course of European colonization.

This long history of state-committed or sponsored mass killings continued, as we know, into current times. The twentieth century, in fact, sought to outdo many of its predecessors. And, in the course of the twentieth century, warfare changed such that the percentage of civilian casualties increased from 14 in World War I to 67 in World War II and up to 90 in the century's final decades (Keegan 1976; Hagan and Rymond-Richmond 2009: 63f).

Have atrocities always been crimes?

No doubt, the behaviors sketched so far have brought immense suffering, pain, hunger, blood, death, tears, and mourning over humankind. But who specifically are the perpetrators? The killers who got their hands bloodied; middlemen who passed on directives; intellectuals who provided the ideological groundwork; or political and military leaders who thought out, motivated and ordered campaigns of destruction? Even if we can agree on whom to appropriately identify as perpetrators, historically they were not typically regarded as criminals. More commonly they were celebrated as heroes—and often they maintained these reputations throughout history. A couple of historical examples must suffice. Consider the robbery and abduction of the entire female population of the Sabine tribe. This horror brought over the Sabiners by the early Romans even became part of the founding myth of ancient Rome. Or, take note of the following statement from Homer's *Iliad*, where the Greek Prince Agamemnon of Mycenae challenges his brother, after the conquest of Troy:

> My dear Menelaus, why are you so chary of taking men's lives? Did the Trojans treat you as handsomely as that when they stayed in your house? No; we are not going to leave a single one of them alive, down to the babies in their mothers' wombs—not even they must live. The whole people

must be wiped out of existence, and none be left to think of them and shed a tear (quoted after Rummel 1994: 45).

How is Agamemnon's frequent, although not unanimous, glorification as a hero throughout the millennia possible in light of such genocidal rhetoric? And further, why do even many contemporaries associate glory with the names of Genghis Khan or Charlemagne. No doubt, they built vast empires, but what about the atrocities for which they are responsible, the uncounted innocent civilians who perished under their command? Sociologist Bernhard Giesen (2004) shows how, historically, those on whom "heroes" imposed great sacrifices, "victims" in our contemporary understanding, were discounted or even perceived as evil or "polluted" (*victima* in Latin: those set aside to be sacrificed). Such understanding obviously complements the celebration of victimizers as heroes.

Some actors in modern times believed they could learn lessons from the past, to emerge as heroes from the course of history, no matter the sacrifices they imposed on others. Lenin and Mao Zedong are examples, and they may have partly succeeded. Yet, their reputations as heroes are at least challenged, and the cruelties they inspired are recorded in history books to taint their reputations (e.g., Chang and Halliday 2005). Others who thought they could act like "heroes" of past eras and carry away similar reputations erred radically. Adolf Hitler, for example, in a speech to leading members of his Nazi party proclaimed in August 1939:

> It was knowingly and lightheartedly that Genghis Khan sent thousands of women and children to their deaths. History sees in him only the founder of a state ... The aim of war is not to reach definite lines but to annihilate the enemy physically. It is by this means that we shall obtain the vital living space that we need. Who *today still speaks of the massacre of the Armenians*? (quoted after Power 2002: 23).

And yet, this was but one of Hitler's fundamental misinterpretations of history. In fact, his own actions advanced changes, long underway, that were to defeat his intent and reasoning. These changes, to which we will return below, contributed to the modern definition of atrocities as crimes and of those who executed them as perpetrators. Hitler could have known better. Even before he came to power, domestic orders and international relations had changed in ways that posed challenges— albeit ambivalent ones—to "heroes" of the old style.

What is the role of states vis-à-vis atrocities, and how did it change?

In Western history, beginning in the seventeenth century, government capacity to exert domestic control increased substantially (Bendix 1996). Trade expanded and allowed for the collection of taxes, the build-up of government administrations, standing armies, transportation infrastructure, police apparatuses, courts, prisons, and general education systems. Such increases in state capacity had primarily civilizing consequences where governments themselves were constrained by internal and external controls. Under such circumstances domestic government control contributed to a considerable reduction of violence among citizens. Homicide rates for Sweden, for example, declined from 33 (per 100,000 population) during the fifteenth through seventeenth centuries, through 16 during the first half of the eighteenth century to 1.5 in the nineteenth century, and—in the capital of Stockholm—down to 0.6 in the first half of the twentieth century (Johnson and Monkkonen 1996). The decline in interpersonal violence simultaneously increased the sensitivities of modern individuals toward the experience of violence, part of the long-term civilizing process (Elias 1978; Eisner 2001).

Given these new sensitivities toward violence, actors like Hitler should have understood that massive blood letting would no longer be disregarded in the judgment of history. In fact, the new sensitivities helped finally institutionalize Judeo-Christian traditions with their recognition of victims as innocent (see Christian beliefs in the sacrifice/ victimization of their God). Victimhood, no longer polluting, became a sacred status, independent of national, ethnic or religious membership, and past "heroes" were redefined as perpetrators (Giesen 2004).

Simultaneously, however, growing state capacity can have catastrophic consequences where domestic checks and balances and external controls are lacking. While the history of atrocities may support Thomas Hobbes' (originally Plautus') famous claim that "man is man's wolf," it suggests caution toward his conclusion that humans should delegate their rights to Leviathan, the mighty state so that he may protect them from each other. History shows with frightening clarity that Leviathan, while taking rights, at times becomes the killer himself. And this killer will deploy his deadly tools on a much larger scale than individuals ever could. As law and society scholar Stanton Wheeler stated in his writings on corporate crime, organizations become effective weapons in the hands of criminals (Wheeler and Rothman 1982). What applies to corporations is even more valid for modern states (on the role of the modern state apparatus in the execution of genocide see Hilberg [1961] 2003; Bauman 1989; Horowitz 2002). Cooney (1997) identified a U-shaped relationship between state-building and deadly violence: consistent with Hobbes' expectations state formation in its early stages actually slows violence, but high levels of centralization of state power do cause high human death tolls. In the latter cases nothing may stand in the way of grave atrocities other than international control.

How did international relations change?

Just as changes in the domestic organization of states affected both the likelihood and definition of atrocities, so did international relations. Here one historic event continues to set crucial parameters for the behavior of states toward their populations and for the ways in which we judge such behavior. This European event, the Thirty Years' War (1618–48) and its resolution, profoundly affected international relations into the present era, with massive—albeit ambivalent—consequences for human rights. A brief historical excursion is in place.

The Thirty Years' War began as a religious war between Catholic and Lutheran lands. In 1618, about a century after the Protestant Reformation, the Bohemian population revolted against Ferdinand II of the House of Habsburg, their new and staunchly Catholic king and emperor of the Holy Roman Empire of German Nations. War erupted, and Spain under King Philip II, already 50 years into the "Eighty Years' War" against the Calvinist Republic of the Low Countries, supported the Catholic side. This was significant support, as Spain at the time was considered the world's most powerful nation. On the Protestant side, first Denmark, one of the mightiest kingdoms of Northern Europe, then Sweden under King Gustavus Adolphus intervened on behalf of the predominantly Protestant Northern German principalities. Finally,

Catholic France entered the war on behalf of the Protestant powers, as Louis XIII and Cardinal Richelieu, his head of government, sought to weaken the German nations to the North and Spain to its South. What had started as a religious war had become a plain power struggle among the major European powers.

The war mostly unfolded on German lands, and the toll was terrible. Estimates of population losses vary between 15 and 30 percent for the entire country and up to sixty percent for some regions. Germany's male population is estimated to have been decimated by half. The Swedish armies alone are said to have destroyed 18,000 villages and 1,500 towns. The treatment of the civilian population was no more humane on the Catholic side. For example, the Emperor's General Tilly had all 30,000 inhabitants of Magdeburg massacred when the city in Northern Germany fell after a long siege. Torture and killings by the military, mostly composed of mercenary soldiers, were supplemented by massive losses due to famines and diseases such as typhus and the plague.

The war was resolved by one of the most remarkable events in the history of international diplomacy, the Peace Conference of Westphalia of 1643–48, named after the German region where it was conducted. The resulting Peace Treaty, signed in the city of Münster in 1648, reshaped Europe's political map. And, it created a new understanding of the nation state that was as revolutionary at the time as it was taken for granted until recently. In addition to the establishment of fixed territorial boundaries between states, it was agreed that a country's citizens submit primarily to the rules of their own government, rather than to neighboring religious or secular powers. Simultaneously, the *principle of national sovereignty* was established, outlawing a state's intervention into domestic affairs of other countries (http://www.yale.edu/lawweb/avalon/westphal.htm). The hope was to prevent international warfare; simultaneously, however, domestic populations were left to the mercy of their rulers.

Still at the outset of the twenty-first century, and despite strong countervailing trends, the principle of national sovereignty is firmly established—no matter international outrage about the behavior of national governments. Recent illustrations include Myanmar's military Junta refusing to allow international help workers into the Irrawaddy River delta where more than one million cyclone victims were lacking shelter, water, food, and medical treatment in 2008; or the international community standing by almost helplessly as genocide unfolds before its eyes in the Darfur region of Sudan. Even the 1945 International Military Tribunal in Nuremberg had prosecuted leading Nazi perpetrators for offenses primarily committed in the course of war, not those committed domestically during their pre-war terror regime.

And yet, the consequences of Westphalia were ambiguous. Outlawing border-crossing intervention at least delegitimized border-crossing atrocities. Further, the principle of sovereignty had established a new kind of multi-lateral international diplomatic collaboration. This, combined with growing sensibilities toward physical violence, a redefinition of victimhood, and new nineteenth century humanitarian law, had one predictable result: Nazi Germany's atrocities would fuel the engine of post-World War II international cooperation and interventionism toward the control of grave violations of human rights. Hitler's hope for the forgetfulness of history proved false.

Is there an absolute understanding of atrocities as crimes?

While the evaluation of atrocities throughout history varies substantially, some will insist that we call atrocities "crimes" no matter if the perpetrators were regarded as heroes and the victims as polluted by their contemporaries. For support, they may cite Edwin Sutherland (1940, 1983), the "father" of American sociological criminology. In his groundbreaking work on "white-collar crime," Sutherland concedes that many forms of corporate wrongdoing constitute only administrative offenses, not crimes in the legal sense. Yet, Sutherland argues that such behaviors should be considered crimes, as what motivates them is no different from what motivates ordinary street crimes, while consequences may be manifold more harmful. The one major difference between street crime and white-collar offenses, Sutherland insists, is that corporate law breakers, those who manipulate markets and expose workers and consumers to great risk, are sufficiently powerful to prevent criminalization of their behaviors by the state. What applies to corporations is valid even more when states perpetrate.

This sociological argument to consider atrocities as crimes independently of their official definition is supported, in jurisprudence, by proponents of the natural law tradition. Rooted in ancient Greek thought, natural law proposes a notion of unalienable individual rights. No doubt, perpetrators of mass killings are law breakers and criminals from this perspective, no matter where in the world and when in human history they commit their offenses.

This author obviously agrees with the argument that atrocities (or corporate wrongdoing for that matter) have disastrous consequences, and may be driven by similar motives as other crimes; that they should be studied by scholars and rejected by ethicists and society at large, no matter if governments recognize them as crimes. Yet, I suggest that we call only those behaviors crime that governments and law have in fact criminalized. I further prefer to call only those behaviors HR violations that HR regimes have recognized as such. In line with the powerful labeling and constructivist traditions in criminology, I think it useful to distinguish between cruelties that are recognized as crimes and those that are not recognized as such (Becker 1963). They may be similar or identical in terms of motivation and consequences, but classical Chicago sociologist W.I. Thomas was right with his famous dictum that what humans define as real becomes real in its consequences.

In conclusion, atrocities are a mainstay of much of human history. Yet, it is only in recent history that conditions exist under which perpetrators should no longer expect to go down in history as heroes and under which victims can attain sacred status. Changes in the formation of states and in international relations, beginning around the seventeenth century, set the stage for the definition of atrocities as crimes, albeit ambiguously and via the detour of state sovereignty. The actual criminalization of atrocities took off in the course of the late nineteenth and twentieth centuries, under very specific cultural and political conditions, a development toward which we turn next.

TWO

how and why have states and governments been constrained?

A review of the development of humanitarian law (HL) and human rights (HR) law reveals their growing universalization and a recent attribution of criminal liability to individuals. We seek to explain each of these trends by examining changes in global civil society and governance.

What changed?

The principle of national sovereignty continues to dominate international law, impeding international intervention when governments abuse domestic populations. Yet, impressive changes in international law are underway (Fichtelberg 2008). They began in the late nineteenth century with one individual's remarkable initiative. Henry Dunant, founder of the International Red Cross, laid the foundation when he worked toward the establishment of the first of a series of international conventions, today known as the Geneva and Hague Convention(s). The Conventions were drafted by multinational conferences, held in the cities after which they are named. They are the:

- *Geneva Convention for the Amelioration of the Condition of the Wounded in Armies in the Field* 1864 (to protect buildings and persons taking care of the wounded; the convention also sought to assure equal medical treatment of all combatants);

- *Second Geneva Convention for the Amelioration of the Condition of Wounded, Sick and Shipwrecked Members of Armed Forces at Sea* 1907;

- *Convention on the Treatment of Prisoners of War* 1929 (to secure humane treatment of POWs, and control mechanisms that guaranteed open information and permit visits to camps by representatives of neutral states);

- *Fourth Geneva Convention Relative to the Protection of Civilian Persons in Time of War* 1949 (rules against the deportation of individuals or groups, the taking of hostages, torture, collective punishment, "outrages upon personal dignity," the imposition of judicial sentences without due-process, and discriminatory treatment).

The Geneva Convention has garnered broad support across the world's nations as is indicated by the large number of 180 signatories (despite exceptions made by then-US President George W. Bush).

While the Conventions set binding international standards for situations of international conflict, they continue to respect national sovereignty. They do not provide mechanisms for intervention in the internal affairs of a country in times of peace, no matter the gravity of humanitarian abuses in a country. Yet, two subsequent Protocols in 1977, marked a weakening of sovereignty.

- Protocol I extended the protections of the Hague/Geneva Conventions to persons involved in *wars of "self-determination,"* typically liberation wars former colonies fought against colonial powers. Violations of humanitarian principles could thus no longer be considered internal affairs of colonizers.

- Going one step further, Protocol II extended humanitarian rights protections to persons involved in *severe civil conflicts*, prohibiting collective punishment, torture, hostage taking, acts of terrorism, slavery, humiliating and degrading treatment, rape, and enforced prostitution.

These Protocols have also found broad support, albeit weaker due to their more interventionist nature, with 150 and 145 signatories respectively.

Humanitarian law is not just symbolic, instead providing a foundation for judicial intervention. Famous examples of trials that drew legitimacy from the Conventions are the International Military Tribunal in Nuremberg (IMT) against leading Nazis and its equivalent, the Tokyo trials against Japanese war criminals, after the end of World War II. Yet, the history of Nazism had shown that even the treatment of domestic populations should not remain unchecked by the international community. Unbearable in itself, mistreatment at home may prepare yet more horrendous offenses against foreign peoples. In Nazi Germany, for example, the gassing of mentally retarded German children and adults served as a training ground for the SS's work on the "final solution" against Europe's Jews and other groups (Schmidt in Heberer and Matthäus 2008). The idea was thus born to extend rights that many countries guaranteed their own citizens (civil rights) to all humans (human rights), independently of their citizenship, and to certify these rights in a covenant and a series of international treaties. Sovereign states would now be bound by a new and growing system of international law that was not limited to times of armed conflict.

An immediate response to Nazi terror was the 1948 Universal Declaration of Human Rights (UDHR). The time was right, not just because of the particular horrors committed by Nazi Germany, but also because Germany had been thoroughly defeated in the war, and its misdeeds could be put on full display. The UDHR was passed by the General Assembly of the newly founded United Nations (UN) on 10 December 1948. Part one, primarily backed by Western countries, guarantees civil and political rights, including rights to free speech, religion, property, fair trials, or protection against cruel punishment, similar to the Bill of Rights of the American Constitution. Part two, pushed by socialist countries, focuses on economic rights and principles of social justice, including the right to work, social security, health care, free education, and reasonable limitations to working hours.

Just one day before the UDHR was passed in San Francisco, another important convention was approved by representatives of 50 nations in Paris: The Convention on the Prevention and Punishment of the Crime of Genocide. It finally came into force on 12 January 1951, having been ratified by 20 nations. Again, one individual played a crucial role: Raphael Lemkin, a Polish lawyer and Jew who had fled Poland during the German occupation, while losing his family in the Holocaust (see Power 2002: 17–78). Lemkin had also, over the years, developed the concept of genocide until it was defined in Article 2 of the Genocide Convention as:

> ... any of the following acts, committed with the intent to destroy, in whole or in part, a national, ethnical, racial or religious group, such as:
>
> Killing members of the group;
>
> Causing serious bodily or mental harm to members of the group;
>
> Deliberately inflicting on the group conditions of life calculated to bring about its physical destruction in whole or in part;
>
> Imposing measures intended to prevent births within the group;
>
> Forcibly transferring children of the group to another group.

Genocide, thus defined, "whether committed in time of peace or in time of war, is a crime under international law which ... [the Contracting Parties] undertake to prevent and to punish" (Article 1). Threatened with punishment are "constitutionally responsible rulers, public officials or private individuals" (Article 4). Clearly, the most serious type of human rights violation was now a crime, in behavioral and in positive law terms (http://www.unhchr.ch/html/menu3/b/p_genoci.htm).

After slow progress in the early decades following the post-World War II efforts, initiatives accelerated again in the late twentieth century. Conventions went into force, for example on the protection of women (1979), children (1990) and indigenous peoples (1991) (see: http://www1.umn.edu/humanrts/instree/ainstls1.htm). Among these later initiatives, however, only the Convention against Torture and Other Cruel, Inhumane and Degrading Treatment or Punishment (1987) applies standards of criminal liability, like the Genocide Convention and HL before it and the Treaty of Rome a few years later.

Despite such progress, a recent review of the history of international human rights law and its enforcement by political scientist and leading human rights researcher Kathryn Sikkink (2009), cautions us: enforcement of the growing number of international treatises tends to be weak. Treaty bodies created by the UN General Assembly, such as the Human Rights Council (www.unhchr.ch/html/menu2/6/hrc.htm), supported by the UN High Commissioner for Human Rights (www.ohchr.

org/EN/Pages/WelcomePage.aspx), focus on states' legal accountability, monitoring violations and work toward solutions with the accused governments, but with few enforcement powers. New regional courts, such as the European Court of Human Rights, the African Court of Human Rights, and the Inter-American Court of Human Rights also apply a state accountability model. Treaty bodies and courts ask states to provide remedies when violations are recorded, including changes in policies and/or reparation payments to individuals victimized by past policies.

Only in the 1990s did a new model of criminal liability begin to supplement state accountability. It was motivated by the atrocities of the Balkan wars and the Rwandan genocide, and enabled by shifts in the international balance of power after the break-up of the Soviet Union and the end of Communism in Eastern Europe (Hagan and Levi 2005). This model initially took the shape of ad hoc tribunals such as the International Tribunal for the former Yugoslavia (ICTY) in The Hague and the International Criminal Tribunal for Rwanda (ICTR). In the late 1990s, however, the Rome Statute of the International Criminal Court was passed. The International Criminal Court (ICC) is "an independent, permanent court that tries persons accused of the most serious crimes of international concern ..." (http://www.icc-cpi.int/about.html). The ICC treaty entered into force on 1 July 2002, and it was joined by 105 nations by October 2008. It is constrained by its jurisdiction over just a small number of especially grave human rights violations (see Chapter 6) and by the refusal of powerful nations such as the US to join.

The creation of new legal institutions corresponds with an increase in trial activity, at the domestic and international levels, from about 70 human rights trials (1979–84) to some 300 such trials (2000–04), the most recent years of a systematic count (Sikkink 2009). More than one third of trials were held in Latin America, and most trials were *domestic trials*, conducted for local human rights abuses (N = 250). Examples include the Argentinean trials against members of the military junta and Iraqi trials against Saddam Hussein and members of his regime. Comparatively few trials are *foreign trials*, held in one country for offenses committed in another country (N = 25) or *international trials* conducted under the auspices of an international court, typically acting on behalf of the UN (N = 20), such as cases before the ICTY and the ICTR. Finally, hybrid models, involving domestic and international features, are exemplified by trials in Cambodia, Sierra Leone, and the former East Timor. The predominance of national courts does not mean, however, that the international realm is unimportant in the realization of human rights law. First, domestic courts apply not only domestic, but also international law. Second, international courts serve as crucial back-up institutions without which much domestic enforcement would not occur (Sikkink 2009; Roht-Arriaza 2005).

In short, the principle of state sovereignty, established by the 1648 Peace Treaty of Westphalia, began to weaken with the development of HL and HR law, initially in the late nineteenth century, and more decisively in the post-World War II era. Specifically, the growing albeit cautious openness toward international intervention into domestic affairs comprises three processes:

> A universalization or globalization of human rights law, its institutionalization in international doctrines and organizations, including courts of law, and its application by many nations in domestic courts;

> An individualization of human rights law, allowing for grievances to be directed not just against governments or entire countries, but also against individuals acting on behalf of these countries (and filed by individuals); and

> A partial criminalization of human rights law, supplementing compensatory mechanisms with penal responses.

How can these trends toward interventionism, the globalization of HR regimes, individualization of enforcement, and criminalization be explained?

Why a globalization of human rights norms?

Globalization has been one of the dominant trends since the later part of the twentieth century. National economies became ever more interwoven through the flow of capital, goods, and workers across national boundaries. Modern communication and transport enhanced encounters between people from diverse national and cultural backgrounds. Meanwhile, international governmental organizations (IO) such as the UN and its many sub-organizations such as the UN Educational, Scientific, and Cultural Organization (UNESCO) proliferated, as did International Non-Governmental Organizations (INGOs), representing a form of civil society at the global level.

On the civil society side Transnational Advocacy Networks (TANs), conceptualized in the path-breaking work of Keck and Sikkink (1998), took on crucial functions. A TAN consists of non-state actors, interacting with each other, with states and with IOs. Bound together by shared values and ideas and a dense exchange of services and information, each network addresses a specific issue such as child soldiering (Rosen 2007) or female genital cutting (Boyle 2003). Dating back to the nineteenth century, TANs expanded massively in recent decades. In the late 1990s five times as many organizations worked on human rights as in 1950 (about one fourth of all INGOs). Today famous INGOs such as Amnesty International, Physicians for Human Rights and Doctors without Borders play crucial roles as constituent members of TANs. TANs are most likely to emerge when channels between domestic organizations and their governments are blocked, typically by the common refusal of repressive regimes to listen. Keck and Sikkink call this a boomerang effect through which grievances from local activists are communicated via transnational NGOs and networks back to the governments of the aggrieved population.

Not being powerful themselves, TANs typically use information, ideas and strategies to alter the information and value orientations of the world around them. Strategies include information politics (to tie networks together and to affect political actors), symbolic and leverage politics (mobilization of shame against powerful corporations or governments), and accountability politics (to convince governments to change their rhetoric on an issue, and, once successful, to hold them accountable). A good example of the latter is the signing of the Helsinki Accords by the Communist countries under Soviet domination in 1975. Intended by these governments as a symbolic, and seemingly cheap, gesture, human rights organizations, media and other governments could later contrast actual behavior with the norms established by the accord to brand the offenders. The effectiveness of TANs is highest when issues involve bodily harm to vulnerable populations, consistent with criminological findings on the perceived seriousness of corporate crime (Schrager and Short 1980); when responsibility can be attached to specific actors; when networks are dense, involving many actors and providing reliable information flow; and finally when target actors show material or normative vulnerabilities. Examples are states that depend on foreign investment or corporations that depend on sympathy and trust among consumers to sell their products.

The emergence of INGOs and their networks can be thought of as the birth of civil society at the global level. Comparable to national civil societies they serve as conduits between global governance institutions and all members of world society. Importantly, they contribute to the creation of global cognitive scripts (or models) and norms, which, once produced, unfold considerable force. Numerous studies conducted in the tradition of world polity theory, show how such scripts orient the behavior of nation states in areas as diverse as education, environmentalism, economic policy, and women's rights (Meyer et al. 1997). Often global scripts explain national policy making better than domestic factors, especially when countries are closely tied to the international community, as signatories of treaties, participants in international conferences or through common membership in international organizations. And again, the more countries depend on the international community in terms of trade or international assistance, the more likely will they pass laws consistent with international expectations.

Specifically for HR the record is mixed. While some studies show how policies passed in compliance with international norms spread and become effective at the local level (e.g., Boyle 2003), Cole (2005) comes to cautionary conclusions. His analysis of data for 130 countries between 1966 and 1999 shows that international ties did promote ratification of the UN political and economic rights covenants. However, democratic constitutions, an internal condition, promoted a country's willingness to sign the "optional protocol," which subjects countries to most rigorous monitoring provisions.

In sum and despite some caveats, globalization and the building of an international civil society have advanced the universal spread of HR regimes.

Why individual criminal accountability?

Penological scholarship has seriously challenged common functionalist approaches that explain criminal punishment through reference to desired outcomes such as deterrence of crime, incapacitation, restitution or rehabilitation (for a masterful review of crucial theories see Garland 1990). Not only do causes of social facts differ from their consequences, but desired outcomes can often be reached through a number of functionally equivalent solutions. In other words, functionalist arguments cannot explain why a penal mechanism was chosen over a therapeutic or compensatory one. Also, empirical cases abound in which either desired outcomes are not achieved, or in which criminal justice policies actually pursue outcomes very different from officially declared goals. Consider totalitarian regimes where criminal punishment becomes a tool for political repression (Savelsberg 1999), and frequent cases of abuse in democracies as well (Manza and Uggen 2006 on felon disenfranchisement in the US). Also the application of international criminal justice is highly uneven, and patterns of punishment are clearly not determined by effectiveness criteria alone. Mighty countries such as China, Russia and the US and their rulers have been spared criminal justice intervention when they offended against HR law. The same applies to smaller countries with cooperative, albeit lawbreaking, governments that are of strategic importance to world powers.

The uneven enforcement of penal law points toward conflict theoretical traditions, where criminal punishment is understood as a mechanism of domination and repression (Rusche and Kirchheimer 2003). But the balance of power must have shifted, if today former or current state leaders face indictments and trials in criminal courts. And it has shifted, given the growing economic interdependence of nations, the emergence of global civil society with its TANs, and the occasional backing of criminal justice intervention by powerful countries or IOs. To be sure, the mobilization of resources on behalf of an international criminal justice system so far has only achieved modest results. For the most part, only *formerly* powerful leaders have been indicted, and their numbers are few (e.g., Charles Taylor and Saddam Hussein; but see Slobodan Milošević and Omar al-Bashir). Mostly, when current officials are prosecuted, they tend to be low ranking officers, internationally and nationally, as the American cases of My Lai in the late 1960s and the recent prisoner abuse and torture case of Abu Ghraib illustrate. HR-oriented criminal justice is thus a far cry from the model of "governing through crime" (Simon 2007) or from the tight disciplinary regime that French thinker Michel Foucault (1975) depicts.

While power relations thus matter in the application of criminal punishment, cultural forces are similarly crucial. Punishment and society scholar David Garland (2001) and cultural sociologist Philip Smith (2008) stress the ever present role, and recent intensification, of public input into criminal justice processes, with non-rational, emotional forces, including the vengeance motive, and the growing role of non-professionals. They alert us to "penal populism," where criminal punishment is no longer understood as the rational application of disciplinary knowledge but as a didactic exercise. As a speech act in which society talks to itself about its moral identity, criminal justice signifies, through the rituals of court trials, the sacred versus the evil. Smith builds his argument on ideas by classical sociologist Emile Durkheim for whom cultural systems evoke emotional reactions when sacred goods are violated. Durkheim also alerts us to one good that is of crucial importance to HR scholarship: the modern "cult of the individual" demands that individuals be treated with respect:

> The human person, by reference to the definition of which good must be distinguished from evil, is considered as sacred, in what can be called the ritual sense of the word. It has something of that transcendental majesty which the churches of all times have accorded to their gods. It is conceived as being invested with that mysterious property which creates a vacuum about holy objects, which keeps them away from profane contacts and which separates them from ordinary life … . Such a morality is therefore not simply a hygienic discipline or a wise principle of economy. It is a religion of which man is, at the same time, both believer and god (Durkheim, quoted after Smith 2008: 18).

The status of an individual's dignity in modern society, also stressed by Erving Goffman, has important consequences for punishment. While it sets limits to the intensity and types of punishment, it simultaneously encourages the punishment of killers, including dictators who radically disregard the "sacred" status of individuals in modern society.

Again, it was just one of Hitler's many blunders when he thought that a modern dictator could act, with impunity, like Ghengis Khan. In light of the newly acquired "sacred" status of the individual, Hitler's actions and those of his followers evoked responses that created a universal cultural trauma, further advancing global consensus regarding the dignity of individuals. Jeffrey Alexander illustrates for post-Holocaust history how, through symbolic extension of the Shoah and psychological identification with the victims, members of a world audience became traumatized by an experience that they themselves had not shared. This generalization began with the legal proceeding of the IMT in Nuremberg, the UN General Assembly's Resolution 95 that recognized Nuremberg, and the UDHR. In the consequence, at least "'customary law' was developed that militated against nonintervention in the affairs of sovereign states when states engage in systematic human rights violations" (Alexander in Alexander et al. 2004: 251). The punishment of leading Nazi perpetrators by the IMT and by subsequent trials (Heberer and Matthäus 2008) was performative or demonstrative in Durkheim's (1961) terms. It provided, consistent with a semiotic model of social life, images, symbols, totems, myths, stories, and it thus contributed to the formation of a collective memory of evil to which we shall return below.

Once established as universal evil, the Holocaust served "analogical bridging" to reinterpret later events in light of this earlier trauma (Alexander in Alexander et al. 2004: 245–9). Examples are the treatment of minorities in the US or the victimization of millions in the Balkan wars during the 1990s. In the latter case, analogical bridging occurred most expressively through the image of an emaciated Bosnian concentration camp inmate behind barbed wire, published on the front pages of most international newspapers. It advanced diplomatic and military intervention and the establishment of the ICTY, with considerable potential at universalizing the case and contributing to new international criminal law (Hagan 2003).

The weight of cultural forces toward establishing criminal justice responses does not mean that conflict, power and institutional context become irrelevant. Power continues to matter when world and military leaders are indicted and tried or when they go free. Power is crucial, when perpetrators are to be arrested, as the offer of incentives and threat of sanctions by the European Union against Serbia illustrated. It was under such pressure that Serbia handed former President Milošević and Bosnian-Serb leader Radovan Karadžić over to the ICTY. And it was the use of power based on force that allowed the American military to arrest General Krstić and others in Bosnia. Finally, power is also crucial when mighty actors set up institutions of international law. Legal scholar Noah Feldman applies this insight to the 2008 US Supreme Court decision that overruled the Bush administration's policies on Guantánamo Bay:

> Law comes into being and is sustained not because the weak demand it but because it is a tool of the powerful—as it has been for the United States since World War II at least. The reasons those with power prefer law to brute force is that it regularizes and legitimizes the exercise of authority. It is easier and cheaper to get the compliance of weaker people or states by promising them rules and a fair hearing than by threatening them constantly with force … (Feldman 2008: 66).

And yet, as classical sociologist Georg Simmel ([1908] 1968) and historian E.P. Thompson (1975) have stressed, once established, legal institutions also constrain the powerful.

In short, human rights norms have become universalized and individual penal liability has been introduced against perpetrators. Shifts in international power, the rise of global organizations and of a global civil society, and the growing sanctity of individual life turn out to be driving forces. Before closely examining penal and other institutional responses, we first inquire into the nature of those acts against which the newly blossoming interventionism in international criminal law is directed. Understanding them is a prerequisite to developing appropriate responses.

PART II
What can criminology contribute to (and learn from) the study of serious human rights violations?

After a brief description of the most meticulously planned—and one of the deadliest—genocides, the Holocaust (Chapter 3), I juxtapose prominent explanations offered by genocide scholars with criminological theories (Chapter 4). Chapter 5 presents a recent effort to apply criminological ideas on crime as collective action to genocide (Darfur) and an organizational criminology perspective to the My Lai massacre.

THREE

how does genocide unfold?—
the case of the Holocaust

Introduction

Having been deeply involved in the production of false test reports for an Air Force airline brake system at the B.F. Goodrich Co. in 1968, Kermit Vandivier remembers: "During that month Lawson [a fellow employee] and I talked of little else except the enormity of what we were doing. The more involved we became in our work, the more apparent became our own culpability. We discussed such things as the Nuremberg trials and how they related to our guilt and complicity …" (Vandivier in Ermann and Lundman 2002: 159). Seven years earlier, in 1961 Judge J. Cullen Ganey read a statement prior to imposing sentences against several General Electric executives for their and their Westinghouse colleagues' engagement in a major price-fixing case: "… they were torn between conscience and an approved corporate policy, with the rewarding objective of promotion, comfortable security, and large salaries. They were the organization or company man, the conformist who goes along with his superiors and finds balm for his conscience in additional comforts and security of his place in the corporate set-up" (Geis in Ermann and Lundman 2002: 122).

Both Vandivier's conversations about Nuremberg and judge Ganey's statement date back to the 1960s, the decade in which many years of relative silence about the Holocaust finally ended and Adolf Eichmann, the chief organizer of the deportations to the Nazi extermination camps was tried in a Jerusalem court, a decade also in which that trial prompted Hannah Arendt (1964) to coin the word about the "banality of evil." Arendt meant to express how simple obedience to bureaucratic routine contributed to the most horrifying genocide of the century. Simultaneously, psychologist Stanley Milgram (1965) published findings from his famous experiment: ordinary Americans too obeyed orders even when they believed that doing so caused intense pain and risked the death of their victims.

Important questions arise. Is what explains genocide and other serious human rights offenses comparable to what causes white-collar crime or crime generally? Would the employees and managers at Goodrich, General Electric and Westinghouse or the subjects in Milgram's experiments have, under different circumstances, contributed to much greater evil as well? And, would author and readers of this book have acted differently from the torturing South African police officer, the common soldier Drazen Erdemović in Bosnia, or the American men from Company C when they killed hundreds of innocent civilians in My Lai? Would they have followed orders to contribute to the genocides of the twentieth century had they found themselves subject to one of the regimes under which these crimes were perpetrated?

And, on a different front, if answers to these questions elicit an at the least qualified "yes" or "maybe," why does criminological literature, especially on organizational crime on the one hand, and political science and historical literatures on serious human rights (HR) violations on the other, not take note of each other? Clearly, such segmentation of knowledge has problematic consequences for our understanding of atrocities and crime generally.

In describing the Holocaust, we follow the steps through which German society produced a genocidal regime and put genocide into practice under that regime. We end with a close look at the contribution of one police battalion.

The Holocaust, or—in Hebrew—Shoah, committed by Nazi Germany against Europe's Jews and the killing of millions of other defenseless victims, especially Poles, Soviet prisoners of war, homosexuals, Sinti and Roma, the mentally and physically handicapped, and political opponents has attracted more scholarship than any other atrocity. The Holocaust is obviously of a different order than the Srebrenica or My Lai massacres and other grave human rights violations introduced at the outset. First, it is on a radically different scale. Second, here the massive killing of entire categories of people was not an unintended or just accepted by-product of war, but the explicit mission of the murder machine. Third, millions of victims of the mass killing were defined exclusively by their ethnic (and presumed racial) group membership—irrespective of their nationality or political leanings. Many Jewish victims were German citizens, had contributed to their country's fame as jurists, artists or scholars, and had fought "for" their country in the trenches of World War I. Fourth, much of the mass murder was committed in a systematically planned and quasi-industrial process of which only a modern society is capable. Fifth, it was committed by a nation that had been considered a leader in modern civilization, culture and science.

I selected the Holocaust for a case study for several reasons. First, although it is universally known, teaching about the Holocaust frequently shows considerable ignorance among students. Second, the Shoah has attracted more scholarship than any other genocide, material that can be conveniently linked to some of the better known criminological explanations of crime. Third, the German crimes of World War II resulted in the first international criminal trials against perpetrators of humanitarian law (HL) and human rights (HR) violations (see Part III). Finally, and this is a personal reason, this author's adult life has been accompanied by a constant engagement with the Shoah.

How did the Nazis come to power and how did the Holocaust unfold?

In 1924, failed artist and World War I veteran Adolf Hitler wrote his infamous book *Mein Kampf*, filled with intense anti-Semitic rhetoric, while serving time in prison for an attempted coup in the German state of Bavaria. In July 1932 the German electorate gave Hitler's Nazi Party 37.8 percent and in November 33.1 percent of the vote. This was a major success for a party that in the 1920s had achieved only single digits (2.6 percent of the vote in 1928). Their percentage of the vote was noticeably higher (18.3 percent) following the onset of the Great Depression. Their representation was higher yet after the November 1932 election; Adolf Hitler was now the leader of the strongest faction in the highly splintered Reichstag (the German legislature). Following the election victory, on 30 January 1933, President Paul von Hindenburg named Hitler chancellor of Germany. These were the last free elections of the Weimar Republic, the first German democratic state, established shortly after the end of World War I. On 27 February 1933 the Reichstag building in Berlin went up in flames—a Dutch Communist was picked as the presumed culprit, and a decree proclaimed severely restricting civil liberties and leading to the arrest of many Communist and other, mostly leftist, opponents of the Nazis. With parts of the opposition disabled, the Nazi Party won 43.9 percent of the vote in 3 March elections. Barely three weeks later, on 23 March, the Nazis, supported by other rightist and conservative parties, used the general paranoia to pass the Enabling Act (*Ermächtigungsgesetz*), allowing the cabinet to decree laws without approval by the legislature for a period of four years—more than enough time for Hitler to set up a totalitarian dictatorship. Already in March 1933 the government began to build the first concentration camp in Dachau just outside of Munich, initially primarily for political opponents. In July 1934 Buchenwald near Weimar was to follow; and in 1936 Sachsenhausen near Berlin, built by inmates of a smaller camp while the international community of athletes prepared for the opening of the Olympic Games in Berlin.

Now the Hitler government had free rein to put its ideologies and racist programs into action. On 7 April 1933 the "Law for the Restoration of the Professional Civil Service" forced all Jewish civil servants out of office. Two months later, a decree expelled all those married to Jews from civil service positions. It took another two and a half years until the Nazi government, on 15 December 1935, passed the infamous "Law for the Protection of German Blood and German Honor," the so-called Nuremberg Law. This law and numerous subsequent decrees set up a detailed system of racial categories, simultaneously outlawing marriages and sexual relationships between Jews and non-Jewish Germans.

Another event, seemingly small, viewed together with the flow of initiatives was to contribute to the pending catastrophe. In 1938, at the request of a father in Leipzig, Hitler had his personal physician travel to visit a severely handicapped child. Agreeing that the child would be a burden on family, and nation, the physician authorized the child's killing. This was the first step toward a vast "euthanasia" program of murdering all who were deemed carriers of genetically transmitted mental and physical handicaps, first children and subsequently adults. This program soon introduced the killing of groups of victims in gas chambers in numerous sites, including the infamous mental health institute of Hadamar near Frankfurt. Simultaneously hundreds of thousands of German women were forcibly sterilized.

On 9 November 1938, the Nazi Party initiated the so-called Night of Broken Glass (Reichs-Pogrom-Night) in which synagogues and Jewish businesses were ransacked. Subsequent decrees deprived Jews of holding driver's licenses, admission to theatres, concert halls, and exhibitions, and from access to sleeping and dining cars on trains.

War was the next step on the path toward genocide. On 1 September 1939 the German army attacked Poland from the West while the Soviet Army occupied the Eastern part of that country. Parts of Czechoslovakia had already been annexed, and Austria had been incorporated into the Third Reich in 1938. Soon several Northern and Western neighbors, including France, were attacked and conquered. Finally, in June 1941, despite a non-aggression treaty between Hitler and Stalin, Hitler ordered the invasion of the Soviet Union. The Soviet-occupied parts of Poland were quickly conquered and the German army progressed to the outskirts of Leningrad and Moscow in just a few months. Yet, the initial "euphoria of victory" (Browning 1998) dissipated quickly as further military progress came to an abrupt halt. However, the brutal repression of Jews in the occupied territories, begun at the outset of the war, would soon reach its climax.

Meanwhile, Western Poland had been incorporated into the Reich, and central Poland, a territory with a vast Jewish population of more than two million, had been reorganized into the so-called *Generalgouvernement*. Jews in the occupied territories were forced to wear the yellow Star of David. They were subsequently concentrated in vastly overcrowded ghettos with miserable living conditions and high death rates. In June 1941, following the "Commissar Order," units of the SS, the Nazi party's own troops, so-called *Einsatzgruppen* began the systematic killing of Soviet officials and "Jews in the service of the Party or State" (Weitz 2003: 127).

The orders were interpreted liberally and soon entire ghettos and villages were "cleared" and the population, first men, then also women and children were shot to death. Simultaneously, in July 1941 a *Generalplan Ost* (Masterplan East) was passed intending to depopulate vast areas and repopulate them with ethnic Germans. Clearly this was not a typical military occupation but a colonization program, and one with particularly brutal treatment of the domestic population (Zimmerer 2005). Soon after the attack on the Soviet Union German Jews were forced to wear the yellow Star of David as a marker on their clothes, like Jews in the occupied territories before them, followed by their systematic deportation to concentration and extermination camps.

While hundreds of thousands of lives would have been extinguished at any rate, millions might have been saved, at least in the short run, if the original plan of a massive resettlement of local populations, including Jews, beyond the Ural Mountains had not failed with the stalling of the war effort on the eastern front. Instead, on 26 January 1942, a group of leading Nazi Party and SS members were joined by several second-rank bureaucrats from crucial *Reichs*-Departments in a mansion on the Wannsee lake on the outskirts of Berlin ("Wannsee-Conference") to formally decide the "final solution"—the systematic annihilation of Europe's Jews. Participants still avoided the use of terms that would have most appropriately described the plan as the following quotation from the minutes illustrates:

> *Another possible solution of the problem has now taken the place of emigration, i.e. the evacuation of the Jews to the East, provided the Führer agrees to this plan.* (Pencilled underlining in original German carbon copy; underlined in English translation.) Such activities are, however, to be considered as provisional actions, but practical experience is already being collected which is of greatest importance in relation to the future final solution of the Jewish problem. Approximately 11,000,000 Jews will be involved in this final solution of the European problem, they are distributed as follows among the countries [Numbers follow broken down by 34 countries or regions.] ... Under proper guidance the Jews are now to be allocated for labor to the East in the course of the final solution. Able-bodied Jews will be taken in large labor-columns to these districts for work on roads, separated according to sexes, in the course of which a great part will undoubtedly be eliminated by natural causes. The possible final remnant will, as it must undoubtedly consist of the toughest, have to be treated accordingly, as it is the product of natural selection, and would, if

liberated, act as a bud cell of a Jewish reconstruction ... In the course of the practical execution of the final settlement of the problem, Europe will be cleaned up from the West to the East ... (quoted in Joods Historisch Museum Amsterdam 1969: 30).

In light of the blocked passage to the East, and the limits of the mass shootings of the populations of entire villages and ghettos, the Nazi regime became "inventive" (Hilberg [1961] 2003). Having learned from the "euthanasia" program, gassing was introduced and extermination camps were set up in Eastern Europe. Already in December of 1941 killings by gas began in the Polish town of Chelmno where the victims were herded into closed trucks, specifically designed in Germany's industrial heartland, and killed by the exhaust fumes on the way to their mass graves. The method had previously been "tested" on Soviet prisoners of war. Five additional extermination camps were set up: Bełćek, Sobibór, Majdanek, Treblinka and Auschwitz. All were connected with the European rail systems and had massive industrial capacities (for an interactive map see: http://www1.yad-vashem.org/education/MainCamps/eng1.htm). The ghettos in the nearby occupied territories were "cleared." Jews from all over Europe's occupied lands were horded into trains. Most of those who survived the days of transport, typically in crammed cattle carts, in extreme heat and cold, with total lack of food and drink, were forced to undress, herded into the gas chambers, and killed by the dozens or hundreds at a time. The corpses were then transported by other victims, forced to their gruesome task, to nearby mass graves or to adjacent ovens and burnt, their ashes dumped into rivers. In the meantime, the mass shootings continued elsewhere. The following year was the most murderous: "In mid-March 1942 some 75 to 80 percent of all victims of the Holocaust were still alive, while 20 to 25 percent had perished. A mere eleven months later, in mid-February 1943, the percentages were exactly the reverse. At the core of the Holocaust was a short, intense wave of mass murder" (Browning 1998: xv). It is estimated that more than 50 percent of the victims perished in the gas chambers of the six major death camps, one quarter in the course of mass shootings and the final quarter through the deadly conditions of ghettos, death marches, and labor and concentration camps (Hilberg [1961] 2003; for an excellent documentary film, based on interviews with surviving victims, perpetrators and witnesses, see Claude Lanzmann's *Shoah*).

Killings on the front lines: a murderous police battalion

One of the most incomprehensible aspects in the unfolding of the Shoah is the capability of men and women to execute the mass killings. They include the staff of the extermination camps and members of units that killed millions of human beings in thousands of mass shootings, mostly special units of the SS. Here we focus on one example, a police battalion that participated in numerous killings of entire ghetto or village populations. This case poses a particular puzzle because the battalion was not staffed with radicalized Nazis and members of the SS but with "ordinary Germans." The material for our case study is provided by two scholars, historian Christopher Browning (1998) and political scientist Daniel Goldhagen (1996). Both independently analyzed Reserve Police Battalion 101, based on the same German criminal court records of proceedings against some of the Battalion's members in the 1960s.

Reserve Police Battalion 101 was composed of "middle-aged family men of working- and lower-class background from Hamburg. Considered too old to be of use for the German army, they had been drafted instead into the Order Police" (Browning 1998: 1). Browning describes this unit's actions, beginning in the village of Józefów, three weeks after its arrival in occupied Poland. It was still dark on 14 July 1942 when the men mounted their trucks, equipped with weapons and extra ammunition. They reached Józefów at early dawn and gathered around their commander:

> ... Major Wilhelm Trapp, a fifty-year-old-career policeman affectionately known by his men as "Papa Trapp." The time had come for Trapp to address the men and inform them of the assignment the battalion had received. Pale and nervous, with choking voice and tears in his eyes, Trapp visibly fought to control himself as he spoke. The battalion, he said plaintively, had to perform a frightfully unpleasant task. The assignment was not to his liking ... , but the orders came from the highest authorities. If it would make their task any easier, the men should remember that in Germany the bombs were falling on women and children. He then turned to the matter at hand. The Jews had instigated the American boycott that had damaged Germany ... There were Jews in the village of Józefów who were involved with the partisans ... The battalion had now been ordered to round up these Jews. The male Jews of working age were to be separated and taken to a work camp. The remaining Jews—the women, children, and elderly—were

to be shot on the spot by the battalion. Having explained what awaited his men, Trapp then made an extraordinary offer: if any of the older men among them did not feel up to the task that lay before him, he could step out (Browning 1998: 2).

About a dozen men took Major Trapp up on his offer, turning in their rifles and awaiting further orders. Others bailed out later, asking for different assignments, when they began to comprehend the enormity of what they were being asked to do. In this, and other cases, those who withdrew from mass murder were not punished. Two platoons from one of the companies now surrounded the village to prevent escapes. The other units received orders to round up the 1,800 Jews who lived in the village and to gather them in the marketplace. Those too sick to move, infants and resisters were to be killed immediately. In the marketplace the men were to be selected out and sent to a work camp. All others were to be escorted to a forest a few kilometers out of town to be shot. A physician explained how the men needed to shoot to cause immediate death (in later actions much less "care" was invested). The firing squads then led groups of victims into the forest and forced them to lie down on the ground. Groups of officers, lining up behind their victims,

> … placed their bayonets on the backbone above the shoulder blades as earlier instructed and fired in unison … Except for a midday break the shooting proceeded without interruption until nightfall … By the end of a day of nearly continuous shooting, the men had completely lost track of how many Jews they had each killed. In the words of one policeman, it was in any case, "a great number" (Browning 1998: 61).

The dead were left lying in the woods, and the men returned by truck to their barracks in a nearby town. Browning describes their state of mind as "depressed, angered, embittered, and shaken" (Browning 1998:69). They did not discuss the massacre, "by silent consensus," but "repression during waking hours could not stop the nightmares" (Browning 1998: 69).

Many more assignments were to follow. Some of the oldest men were dismissed and returned to Hamburg. The turnover rate was substantial, and by November 1943 only a portion of the officers who had participated in the Józefów massacre was still with the Battalion. Others developed a sense of routine which prepared them for the biggest action, the "harvest festival" massacre of 4 November 1943, in which 42,000 Jews were murdered; the largest single massacre committed by a German unit. Here they did not do the shooting, but they formed "the human cordon through which 14,000 work Jews from Poniatowa, stark naked and hands behind their necks, marched to their deaths while the loudspeaker once again blared music in a vain attempt to cover up the noise of the shooting" (Browning 1998: 140).

After World War II, Major Trapp and three others were extradited to Poland. Trapp and one other officer were sentenced to death and executed, the other two received prison sentences. In Germany, it took until 1958 for the Central Agency for the State Administrations of Justice to be formed to investigate Nazi crimes. Four years later, the Agency forwarded the case regarding Police Battalion 101 to the judicial authorities in Hamburg. Two hundred and ten former members were interrogated, but only fourteen were indicted, and only five unconditional prison sentences resulted. Browning (1998: 146) hopes "… that the admirable efforts of the prosecution in preparing this case will serve history better than they have served justice." This hope may be partially fulfilled, as judicial records can in fact help in the writing of history (Chapter 7).

In short, a highly civilized nation proved capable of bringing to power a genocidal regime; and regime and society cooperated in the execution of genocide, from leaders, planners, bureaucrats, and bystanders all the way down to the executioners. How can the unfathomable be explained? What does the scholarly record say? Can criminology learn from it, and can it contribute?

FOUR

can genocide studies and criminology enrich each other?

After examining challenges in the encounter between criminology and genocide studies, we juxtapose explanations and theories from both fields and ask what they have to offer each other.

What might inhibit communication?

First, criminological vocabulary differs substantially from that used by genocide scholars. While the latter discuss phenomena such as totalitarian and revolutionary regimes, war and social instability, racist and anti-Semitic ideologies, criminologists use concepts such as learning and culture, strain and anomie, social control and social disorganization. And yet, where one school of criminology addresses culture, for example, historians are concerned with specific cultural expressions such as anti-Semitism; and where other criminologists discuss social disorganization or anomie, historians explore the role of crises. At times concepts used are virtually identical such as "neutralization" or "opportunities."

Second, genocide scholars' frequent concern with single cases contrasts with criminologists' typical interest in general patterns. Yet, newer historical-comparative genocide scholarship is moving toward general theory (e.g., Weitz 2003). Also, under the cover of analyzing large single cases there often hide explanations of more general micro- and macro-level phenomena involving group pressure or value orientations or chances that some categories of people are more likely to kill than others, all factors addressed by criminologists.

Third, historians are primarily concerned with past cases while criminologists tend to focus on current-day phenomena. Yet, there is a history of the present (or very recent past), while historical criminology has become an important branch of its field (e.g., Rafter 1988).

Fourth, while criminology often proceeds deductively, testing general theories with empirical data, genocide scholars commonly proceed inductively, weaving together a rich tapestry of empirical findings to arrive at explanations. Yet in practice, elements of induction and deduction typically enrich the work of both historians and sociologist-criminologists.

Fifth, both genocide scholars and criminologists tend to work with different types of data (e.g., archives vs. surveys), but it seems obvious that merging insights from different data sources can only enrich our understanding of social phenomena generally and of grave human rights violations specifically.

Finally, criminologists—even those concerned with the social structure surrounding criminal behavior—focus on individuals and their offenses (or aggregations to rates). This is much in line with the inclination of modern criminal law to attach criminal liability to individuals. Also in line with a criminal law perspective, the state as the creator and enforcer of law is typically excluded as a potential culprit. In both respects, genocide scholars show more independence from a state-centered perspective. They recognize the state as a potential perpetrator, and they bear in mind the multitude of actors and the complexity of processes that potentially culminate in genocide as a form of collective action. Consider the many contributors to the Shoah: Nazi leaders who ordered the genocide; SS-troops who executed most of the killings, supported by police battalions; bureaucrats who kept the auxiliary state machinery running; physicians and lawyers (Stolleis 2007) who provided their expertise to the mass murder; collaborating countries (Fein 1979); bystanders who did not intervene but at times benefited; and voters who had supported the Nazi party in the final Weimar elections of 1932 and 1933.

Each of these types of actors may require specific explanations. Importantly though, all of them were interconnected. Many could not have prevailed if others had not created, or contributed to, the necessary context and preconditions. Bulgarian philosopher Tzvetan Todorov (1995), writing about post-transition responses to concentration camps, argues that the most difficult problem is the passing on of responsibilities. Executioners shift responsibility to ever higher levels, and those at higher levels pass it down to those at the bottom of the hierarchy. This ability of shifting responsibility around is, Todorov argues, a faithful reflection of the *structure of totalitarian crime*. It always involves organizational structures, a dilution of responsibility through radical separation between decision makers and actors on the ground (for the former to keep their hands clean, for the latter their conscience clean). Given such fragmentation, Todorov argues one cannot condemn just one piece of totalitarianism—a challenge not just to judicial responses but also to any explanation of totalitarian crimes.

These are central lessons for criminology. Grave human rights violations can only be understood as the outcome of collective or organizational, especially state, action. While individuals perpetrate, their actions alone can never account for the gruesome outcome.

What happens when Holocaust scholarship and criminology meet?

Further insights can be gained when we juxtapose prominent explanations of genocide with criminological theories. The aim here cannot be a comprehensive review, but an illustration of potentials and limits by way of selecting classic themes and theories from both branches of scholarship. From criminology I initially consider basic micro- and macro-level approaches as they address opportunities (control and disorganization), motivation (learning and culture), clashes between structure and culture (strain and anomie), and power imbalances. Again, comparing selections from two huge bodies of literature in very limited space can only be a first step, and it will require some patience from specialists on each side. Yet, each side should learn from this juxtaposition. We advance from the micro- to the macro-analytical level.

Personalities?

Are perpetrator peoples characterized by particular personalities? Early arguments, such as Theodor Adorno's emphasis on the role of an "authoritarian personality" to explain the Nazis' success in Germany have been thoroughly challenged. Empirical evidence suggests that humans generally are capable of at least being bystanders in the midst of brutality. Bystanders, sociologist Everett Hughes (1963) argued have an especially easy time in modern societies where specialized staff takes care of the "dirty work." They accept the definition of a situation as a problem and leave the execution of its "solution" to a small group of "experts," while closing their eyes to the brutalities exerted by these groups.

Those who conduct the "dirty work," however, are most likely to be recruited from "... men or women with a history of failure, of poor adoption to the demands of work and of the classes of society in which they had been bred. Germany between wars had large numbers of such people. Their adherence to a movement which proclaimed a doctrine of hatred was natural enough ..." (Hughes 1963: 33). Hughes' arguments, based on observations in Germany shortly after the end of World War II, are radicalized by the lessons psychologist Philip Zimbardo (2007) drew from experimental research. In his famous Stanford Prison Experiment (1970) he divided research subjects into a "guard group" and a "prisoner group." He was cautious, excluding potential research subjects who scored beyond normal on psychological tests regarding rigid adherence to traditional values and submission to authority. Still, Zimbardo found that, within days, the guard group, normal young people in all respects, commonly engaged in brutality, humiliation and dehumanizing treatment toward the "prisoners." Browning (1998), comparing his research on Police Battalion 101 with Zimbardo's findings, discovered an interesting parallel: about one third of both the police officers and Zimbardo's test groups emerged as *particularly* "cruel and tough."

The conclusion is frightening then. Ordinary humans can become bystanders to and even practitioners of atrocities. Special personalities are not required. But obviously and gratefully, most humans never engage in such actions and others only under specific circumstances. The focus is then directed toward the conditions under which people turn into Zimbardo's "guards" or, returning to a previous metaphor, Hobbes' famous "wolf."

Group dynamics?

As atrocities are typically carried out in the context of groups, do groups induce persons with normal personality features to engage in atrocities? Scholars see different types of atrocities, each with its specific group processes. Collins (2008: 99), for example, distinguishes "forward panics," that is atrocities growing out of situations of intense fear and tension, from atrocities that follow deliberate orders from high military or political authorities. Related, Browning refers to the latter as standard operating procedure, distinguishing them from battlefield atrocities.

Obviously, the mass killings of the Holocaust are "standard operating procedure." And yet, while the orders came from above, the immediate group context helps explain why 80 to 90 percent of the officers in Police Battalion 101 followed the orders and engaged in the shootings they first experienced as repugnant. Browning identifies the following motives: not shooting not only left the "dirty work" to the comrades, the only reference group physically available in the field, but also increased the burden on fellow officers by signaling a moral reproach. This argument corresponds with classical research from industrial and military sociology (Stouffer et al. 1949), showing that solidarity and pressure in small groups of co-workers and fellow soldiers are more decisive in determining the actions and engagement of their colleagues than superior orders or ideological directives (also Collins 2008).

And yet, despite orders and group pressure, most "ordinary men" of Police Battalion 101 were gravely troubled by their deeds (Browning 1998). The turn-over rate was high, and in the worst atrocities such as the "harvest festival," the greatest mass killing of the Holocaust, they "only" served as a cordon through which the victims slowly moved toward the execution site, while the shootings were executed by members of the SS.

While ordinary men are thus capable of executing horrendous atrocities, the task can be accomplished most "successfully" where personnel are specifically selected and organized in groups with shared ideological convictions, and provided with opportunities to learn the use of brutalities against fellow humans. Concentration camps, beginning in 1933, became training grounds, places of "apprenticeship," in which SS men—selected on ideological conviction and placed in units of ideologically likeminded—learned to apply bestial brutalities. This was crucial preparation for the later mass murder on the Eastern front and in the extermination camps. Similarly, experimenting with mental patients and killing the mentally handicapped helped medical personnel learn the techniques of mass murder to be applied later in the extermination camps (Heberer in Heberer and Matthäus 2008).

Learning in groups?

If learning in social groups with selective membership is one mechanism through which atrocities can be prepared then one link to criminological literature is obvious. Edwin Sutherland, author of America's first "criminology" textbook of 1924 (for the ninth edition see Sutherland and Cressey 1974) and president of the American Sociological Association, stressed early on that crime cannot be explained as a result of individual pathologies. He challenged the personality explanation, arguing instead that crime is learned like any other activity. Sutherland (1940, 1983) demonstrated this insight most convincingly through his analysis of corporate crime, committed by ordinary, well educated, church going members of society who, however, are caught in corporate social environments with deviant standards. His famous proposition is that "[a] person becomes delinquent because of an excess of definitions favorable to violation of law over definitions unfavorable to violation of law" (Sutherland and Cressey 1974: 75). Individuals who get ready for crime (and atrocities) learn values, norms, motivations, justifications, techniques and skills, in differential associations through social reinforcement and validation, like persons in all other realms of social life.

Yet, the study of the Holocaust shows that scholars of genocide must go beyond Sutherland's differential association argument, examining a higher level of social organization where the sources of deviant group standards may be located. First, groups are consciously organized by the state to enhance the learning and execution of "dirty work." Second, the state promotes learning to such groups through massive campaigns, like those of the Ministry for Propaganda in Berlin. Through such methods, the Nazis diffused and reinforced stereotypical images of "the Jew" and simultaneously propagated the "glory" of the Nazi Party and the "Aryan race." Examples are the propaganda films of Leni Riefenstahl on the Berlin Olympics or the Nuremberg Nazi Party Rallies.

Maintaining self-respect?

Participants in atrocities are not just that. They own another self as regular members of civil society, and they have relatives and friends who live normal civilian lives. Given the stark contrast between the norms of everyday life and the engagement in atrocities, participants rely on protective measures to maintain self-respect. Accordingly political scientist Raul Hilberg ([1961] 2003), in his early and seminal study of the Holocaust, stresses that inhibitions, deeply rooted in a long civilizing process, had to be overcome for the killers to pursue their murderous agenda. He quotes an SS-commander: "Look at the eyes of the men of this commando, how deeply shaken they are. These men are finished for the rest of their lives. What kind of followers are we training here? Either neurotics or savages!" (Hilberg [1961] 2003: 1080). Hilberg builds his arguments from here: "Savagery" had to be controlled through disciplinary measures, he argues, and neuroticism through moral techniques. Disciplinary measures included the enforcement of principles such as "All Jewish property belongs to the Reich!" and the prohibition of unauthorized killing. In criminological terms, occupational crime was to be controlled so that organized and organizational crime could be pursued all the more effectively.

But what about the "moral" side of the challenge? How could the perpetrators fulfill their tasks without losing their identity as proper members of humanity? Hilberg describes an arsenal of defenses consisting of mechanisms of repression and ideological and individual rationalization (or neutralization) that is familiar to criminologists (Sykes and Matza 1957; for corporate life Geis in Ermann and Lundman 2002; for concentration camps Sofsky 1996).

Repression included information control, practiced especially toward Jews themselves all the way to the undressing areas outside the "shower rooms" that turned out to be gas chambers, and toward the Axis partners who had coalesced with Nazi Germany. Further strategies included prohibition of criticism, elimination of the destruction process as a subject of social conversation, and language rules. Terms such as "killing" or "killing installation" would be avoided in official communication. Instead, code terms such as "final solution of the Jewish question," "special treatment," "evacuation," or "special installations" were the vocabulary of choice (Hilberg [1961] 2003: 1090; for a literary depiction see Orwell 1949; for "sneaky speak" in a much less brutal, yet torturous setting—the Guantánamo Bay prison camp, see Khan 2008: 176).

Finally, rationalization was pursued through the propaganda machine of the Nazi empire. Jews were depicted as "evil" and Jewish life as a lower form of life, associated with illness and disease. For the broad German public, "documentaries" from overcrowded ghettos in the occupied territories, commissioned by Minister for Propaganda Joseph Goebbels, were shown regularly on newsreel; the appalling conditions of the captured Jews were attributed to them through their own conduct (Friedländer 2007: 19–24). In addition to such propaganda, individual rationalizations also helped participants justify their participation in the destruction process. They included the doctrine of superior orders and, for bureaucrats, the insistence that they did not act out of personal vindictiveness. Tales of "good deeds" for Jewish neighbors abounded and meant to separate "duty" from personal feelings. And finally, common division of labor arguments helped perpetrators save face: I was just one among thousands, and nothing would have happened if those thousands had not acted.

Culture as cause?

Repressive vocabularies, neutralization arguments, and "us versus them" schemas are tools embedded in broader cultural repertoires. Goldhagen (1996) most radically uses a "culture" theme in his book *Hitler's Willing Executioners*. He argues that Germans were not just able, but inclined to execute the Holocaust, and he attributes this eagerness to a particular, enduring national culture. This culture is permeated by a pervasive and "eliminationist" form of anti-Semitism that already in pre-Nazi Germany had "more or less governed the ideational life of civil society" (Goldhagen 1996: 106). Hitler simply had to tap into this reservoir to unleash the genocide. Where Germans were silent bystanders, Goldhagen attributes such silence not to fear, but to approval. And, on the Eastern front, ordinary Germans simply wanted to be perpetrators. Goldhagen's position remindsus, within criminology, of the "culture of violence" tradition where deeply seated and enduring cultures explain engagement in violent crime (Wolfgang and Feracuti 1982).

Browning engages these arguments on methodological and substantive grounds, incorporating much of the scholarly critique evoked since the publication of Goldhagen's book. How could anti-Semitism have been enduring and eliminationist, he asks, given the continuing emancipation of Jews in late nineteenth century Germany (even in periods of repressive measures against Socialists and Catholics) and given the critical attitudes of many Germans toward hooliganistic measures against Jews, for example, the Night of Broken Glass? Browning does acknowledge the role of anti-Semitism though. He also concedes that turn-of-the-century "xenophobic anti-Semitism" turned into a more dangerous "chimeric anti-Semitism" under the impression of the traumatic experiences of World War I, the defeat, the humiliating Versailles Treaty, the period of political violence following the war, the instability of the Weimar Republic and eventually the mass unemployment of the Great Depression. A pre-existing cultural trait thus interacted with a crisis situation to create a sense of prejudice that could indeed be mobilized by Hitler and his chief ideologues. Even then, in occupied Eastern Europe, ordinary Germans still had to be transformed to practice genocide. Groups had to be trained in mass murder. A "culture of cruelty" had to be created in the killing environment. Different from Goldhagen, this type of argument is more in line with criminological thought about culture as a situational adaptation to adverse conditions (Anderson 1994). Yet, going beyond such criminology, Holocaust literature recognizes powerful actors who purposefully exploit structural adversities in order to create a murderous culture.

Sophisticated historical genocide scholarship thus goes beyond a simplistic enduring-versus-situational-culture argument. The complexity of its arguments grows further in works such as historian Saul Friedländer's (2007) *The Years of Extermination: Nazi Germany and the Jews, 1939—1945*. Critical of both Browning's focus on group dynamics and Goldhagen's national culture argument, he weaves together a wealth of historical findings and sources to an 800+ page tapestry. His differentiated depiction stresses four conditions that interacted to make the Holocaust possible: First is indeed a specific kind of anti-Semitism, "Hitler's own brand," a "redemptive anti-Semitism" that portrayed Jews as a lethal and active threat to all nations, especially to Aryans and Germans. And the public, not just in Germany, bought this ideological product: "… the flames that the Nazi leader set alight and fanned burnt as widely and intensely as they did only because, throughout Europe and beyond … a dense underbrush of ideological and cultural elements was ready to catch fire" (xix). To a large degree, this underbrush consisted of the identification of Jews with two sets of ideologies that had for some time mobilized revolutionary right movements: liberalism and revolutionary types of socialism.

Yet, even in this context, highlighted in Germany by challenging post-World War I conditions, Hitler and his helpers had to sell their brand of "redemptive anti-Semitism." They did so through constant ideological mobilization, the second condition for the Holocaust to materialize (Friedländer 2007: xx). This was the mobilizing function of Hitler's image of "the Jew." Third, this image helped maintain Hitler's charisma, the special bond between him and a large segment of the German population as of the mid-1930s. This bond stemmed from the role of Jews in:

> … three different and supra-historical salvation creeds: the ultimate purity of the racial community, the ultimate crushing of Bolshevism and plutocracy, and the ultimate millennial redemption (borrowed from Christian themes known to all). In each of these traditions the Jew represented evil per se. In that sense Hitler's struggle turned him into a providential leader as, on all three fronts, he was fighting against the same metahistorical enemy: the Jew (Friedländer 2007: xx).

Fourth, Hitler was all the more successful, as he simultaneously took into account the vested interests of a diversity of social groups who benefited in direct or indirect ways from the Nazi state's anti-Semitic campaign (on the materialist, bread-and-butter base of the early Nazi movement see Brustein 1996).

Friedländer's cultural argument is thus complex, taking into account ideological mobilization, charisma supported by long-standing salvation creeds and material interest. Recent comparative research shows that the complexity of Friedländer's argument, and some of the central factors he highlights, apply not just to the Shoah but to genocide generally. Historian Eric Weitz (2003), for example, comparing the Holocaust, Soviet mass killings under Lenin and Stalin, the murderous Pol Pot regime in Cambodia, and the atrocities committed in Bosnia, finds three causal factors at work in all four cases: the establishment of linked ideologies of race and nation; the establishment of a revolutionary regime with vast utopian ambitions that involve the model of a "new man," based on ideas of race or class, of "purity" and, citing Durkheimian anthropologist Mary Douglas, the elimination of alien elements as a source of pollution; and, finally, moments of crisis that are generated by war and/or domestic upheaval.

From crises via culture to crime?

If crises are one foundation on which demagogues can build cultures of hatred, then criminology should have contributions to make to the explanation of genocide, albeit after appropriate revisions. Consider two distinct approaches:

First, crises that characterize post-war eras or economic depression are often associated with the breakdown of social ties, family, work and associational life. Criminologists who focus on social disorganization (macro-level) and social control (micro-level), address exactly these types of situations. Assuming criminal motivation as a given, they focus on the lack of ties with legitimate groups and institutions that normally exert social control (Hirschi 1969). Empirical support for this argument reaches back to the old Chicago School of Sociology, where Clifford Shaw and Henry MacKay diagnosed concentrations of crime in neighborhoods with massive geographic mobility and instable social institutions, independently of which ethnic group happened to inhabit those areas. Recently, the Chicago urban neighborhood project confirmed that institutional instability contributes to higher crime rates. Collective efficacy instead, the readiness of community members to activate the norms of the neighborhood against crime, significantly reduces rates of violent crime (Sampson and Raudenbush 1999). Life course research confirms how changing affiliations with legitimate institutions, through marriage or employment, affect the likelihood of criminal offending (Sampson and Laub 1993). Risks deriving from social disorganization are further enhanced when opportunities such as unprotected targets present themselves (Cohen and Felson 1979). One such target, in periods of grave ethnic strife, is minority populations. Criminologists might study how social disorganization in historical crises contributes to not just individual crimes, but to waves of violence and societal destabilization, advancing the rise of authoritarian and racist movements to political power and thus setting the stage for grave repression and possibly genocide.

Second, crises are also periods of uncertain expectations, typically accompanied by a mismatch between desires, needs, or ambitions on the one hand and social, cultural and material opportunities on the other. This mismatch and the resulting tensions have famously been addressed by approaches that focus on "strain" (micro-level) and "anomie" (macrolevel), originating in Durkheimian thought and in Robert K. Merton's (1938) classic work.

A brief excursus is needed for the benefit of non-criminologist readers. Merton famously addressed both aspects of social organization: culture, understood here as basic goals and institutionalized means for attaining them, and structure, the distribution of access to legitimate means such as education, jobs and income. Crime is then explained along two paths. First, when striving for institutionalized goals such as material goods clashes with lacking availability of legitimate means, individuals experience strain and are likely to resort to "innovation," the choice of illegitimate means to achieve highly desired goals. While this argument makes sense in the explanation of "utilitarian" crime, many offenses do not lead to the achievement of institutionalized goals. Instead, and this leads toward a second explanatory path, non-utilitarian crimes have been interpreted as an expression of alternative or oppositional cultures, developed within underprivileged groups, and providing access to status gain through law breaking behavior (e.g., Albert Cohen's (1955) "status frustration" approach). The building of deviant cultures is thus a second way of adapting to strain under conditions of deprivation and crisis.

So far criminologists have applied these theoretical tools primarily to phenomena such as delinquent youth cultures, but certainly not to the emergence of deviant and potentially murderous political cultures. Clearly, much work needs to be invested, but the potential can at least be sketched. Consider the Nazi culture, as it emerged in the post World War I era: high nationalist ambitions had been frustrated by the lost war and the burdening and humiliating Versailles peace treaty; the newly founded first German democracy, the Weimar Republic, was initially marred by violence, partly nourished by economic hardship and by challenges to reintegrate the troops who had returned from the front lines into civilian life (including a private named Adolf Hitler and a fighter pilot named Herman Göring); frustration was further advanced by economic and political instability, a highly splintered political party landscape with continuously changing administrations, and, later, the Great Depression. Collective status frustration then contributed to the emergence and strengthening of a deviant counter-culture with a radical ideology, messages of hate, and promises to return glory to the country, albeit through violent and illegitimate means. At the center of that culture, in the words of Everett Hughes, stood a movement with "… an inner group that was to be superior to all others, even Germans, in their emancipation from the usual bourgeois morality; people above and beyond the ordinary morality" (1963: 33).

Modern state and bureaucracy?

Atrocities, a mainstay of human history, take on a specific shape in light of the capacities that modern states can bring to bear (Bauman 1989; Horowitz 2002). Consider the role of bureaucrats and the bureaucratic machine in the hands of the Nazi state. One example often cited and most infamous is Adolf Eichmann, a former sales representative, SS-member since 1932 and finally Head of the Department for Jewish Affairs in the Central Security Agency in 1939. In this role he became the chief organizer of the transports to the extermination camps. He escaped to Argentina after the war, was kidnapped by the Mossad, the Israeli Secret Service, and put on trial in Jerusalem. The trial and transcripts from the police interrogation prompted political philosopher Hannah Arendt (1964) to coin the term of the "banality of evil." She concluded that Eichmann was not a monster, outside the realm of regular human existence, but a rather ordinary bureaucrat—even though he also proved most inventive whenever the execution of the annihilation plan appeared threatened.

Arendt's view is partially consistent with historian Raul Hilberg's ([1961] 2003) three-volume depiction of the bureaucratic process through which the annihilation was executed: from the definition of future victims via their concentration and on to annihilation. Crucial in this process, and this is Hilberg's central argument, was a well functioning bureaucracy, operating in the context of a totalitarian regime, the secretive plan of Wannsee, and war. Within this context thousands of bureaucrats shared in the "experience" of genocide by fulfilling often ordinary orders. Minutely studying bureaucratic records, Hilberg ([1961] 2003: 1060) finds a "mosaic of small pieces, each common place and lusterless by itself. Yet, this progression of everyday activities, these file notes, memoranda, and telegrams, embedded in habit, routine, and tradition, were fashioned into a massive destruction process. Ordinary men were to perform extraordinary tasks."

But even a well functioning bureaucracy at war faces massive administrative challenges in promoting mass murder. How to overcome them, is part of the explanatory puzzle.

> In the totality of the administrative process, the destruction of the Jews presented itself as an additional task to a bureaucratic machine that was already straining to fulfill the requirements of the battlefronts. One need think only of the railroads, which served as the principle means of transporting troops, munitions, supplies, and raw materials ... Notwithstanding these priorities, no Jew was left alive for lack of transport to a killing center. The *German* bureaucracy was not deterred by problems, never resorting to pretense, like the Italians, or token measures, like the Hungarians, or procrastination, like the Bulgarians. German administrators were driven to accomplishment ... They always did the maximum (Hilberg [1961] 2003: 1076; my emphasis).

In addition to bureaucracy, there is another element—a particularly and tragically functioning *German* bureaucracy, contrasting with bureaucracy of other nations also involved in the Holocaust. The bureaucracy argument is linked with a cultural one, while the sources of that culture are left to further study.

Elements of bureaucracy have also been considered for those who executed the "dirty work" on the front lines. The functional and physical distancing of the bureaucratic machine, so crucial in Hilberg's account, does not offer a satisfactory explanation for the perpetrators on the front lines such as the men in Police Battalion 101. The Battalion's involvement in murder was too direct; its members were "quite literally saturated in the blood of victims shot at point-blank range" (Browning 1998: 162). And yet, some help did arise from the division of murderous labor. In many of the later actions, the battalion's "work" was focused on clearing the ghettos, hording the victims onto freight trains, or forming the cordon through which the victims were led to execution sites, while "specialists" took over the shooting.

And consider obedience to authority, another feature of bureaucracy: while many front line perpetrators did not act out of duress (no one was punished for not killing civilians), a general inclination to obey authority helps explain engagement in atrocities as standard operating procedure. Milgram's (1965) famous experiments had shown, after all, that ordinary American research subjects followed the "researcher's" instructions to expose their victims to intense pain and risk of death. Despite differences between Milgram's experimental conditions and the Police Battalion (where the authority structure was complex and unclear and Major Trapp had offered a way out), distant authorities had left no doubt that they wanted the men to kill. Orders applied in both cases.

Totalitarianism?

The danger that state bureaucracy will be used for genocidal purposes grows immensely when systems of checks and balances break down, when bureaucracy becomes a tool in the hands of highly concentrated political power, and when the political system penetrates into all other aspects of society, that is, in totalitarian states. Rummel (1994) alerted us to the risks of massive concentration of political power while the role of totalitarianism is explored in the work of scholars such as Friedländer, Hilberg, Horowitz and Weitz.

Again, criminology should have contributions to make. First consider the concentration of power. Conflict-theoretical criminology has long highlighted instances where deviance and crime are means through which groups, social classes or states, either resist repression or exploit domination (Chambliss 1989; Kramer and Michalowski 2005; Turk 1982). Charles Tittle (1995) argues that both control deficits and surpluses ("control imbalance") produce deviant behavior. With growing control deficits, deviance first takes the form of predation, then defiance and finally submission. Reports by former concentration camp inmates, exposed to the most extreme control deficits, give frightening testimony (Neurath [1943] 2005). On the other side, growing control surplus increases the chances first of exploitation, then plunder and finally decadence.

> Classic examples [of decadence include] autocratic rulers like Nero who fiddled when Rome burned ... [Plunder is exemplified by] ... environmental pollution inflicted by imperialist countries whose leaders are in search for scarce resources in underdeveloped countries, ... enslavement of natives by invading forces for the benefit of military commanders, ... [and] pogroms through which political or military leaders try to exterminate whole categories of people they find undesirable (as in the Hitler-imposed Holocaust or the devastation of Native Americans by any number of people during the frontier expansion in the history of this country...) (Tittle 1995: 191).

While criminology has started to think about the criminogenic consequences of extreme power concentration, we find little thought on totalitarianism, the radical penetration of the state into all aspects of life. We find guidance, however, in the work of Steven Messner and Richard Rosenfeld (2007) who examine imbalances between institutional sectors of society. Their well known "institutional anomie" model seeks to explain high rates of serious crime in the US: a strongly developed "American Dream" that produces intense pressure for monetary success under conditions of free competition weakens social norms and advances anomie. Further, economic institutions dominate over others (family, education, civil society, polity) that might confine goal attainment to the use of legitimate means. Strongly institutionalized economic principles *devalue* the latter spheres (education is regarded primarily as a means toward occupational attainment, not as an intrinsic good); force them to *accommodate* (minimal family leave policies); and *penetrate* them (the polity resorts to a "bottom line" mentality). Messner and Rosenfeld's model certainly depicts massive institutional imbalance.

Their argument should be reformulated for our purposes as totalitarianism simply represents a different type of institutional imbalance, a superordination of a highly centralized and ideologized political sphere over all other social institutions: non-state institutions are *devalued*, when, for example, "attitude trumps knowledge" (a Nazi saying) in educational institutions. Other spheres are forced to *accommodate*, in the extreme, when voluntary associations have to shut down their operations. Finally, other institutions were *penetrated*, for example, when family members were encouraged to report on relatives to the secret police (Gestapo); when school teachers who did not join the Nazi Party were laid off; when local chapters of the Hitler Youth organization kept a check on "suspicious" school mates; or, when the Party-dominated state replaced the leadership of the German Protestant Church, historically strongly aligned with the Prussian state, with loyal Nazis.

Clearly, under conditions of massive centralization of power and totalitarianism, the state's motivations and opportunities to commit crime amplify, especially once categories of people have been successfully defined as unworthy of life, excluded from the realm of moral obligation (Fein 1979), and once killing installations have been installed. Absolute power not only corrupts, but it generates killers. This principle applies to the system level as well as to specific organizations within the totalitarian state. Consider Franz Ziereis, the commander of the Mauthausen Concentration Camp near the city of Linz, Austria. Ziereis provided his young son with prisoners for live target shooting. He occasionally stood at some distance to randomly select prisoners from newly arrived transports to practice his own shooting skills. He personally engaged in beating up prisoners, and he volunteered to drive those gassing vans in which carbon dioxide was rooted back into the truck to kill the prisoners locked inside (Waller 2007: 5–8). In the likes of Franz Ziereis we encounter individuals, who experience not only absolute power within the camp setting, but simultaneously experience violence as pleasure and thrill (Katz 1988; also Brannigan and Hardwick 2003: 118).

Agency?

None of the factors discussed in this chapter is deterministic, and none of the actors can be easily and fully classified. Auschwitz survivor Primo Levi in his famous essay on "The Grey Zone" (1989), differentiates within the categories of perpetrators and victims. He describes perpetrators who showed mercy and victims who collaborated. Browning agrees, and he sees room for agency that becomes visible among the men of Police Battalion 101:

> The story of ordinary men is not the story of all men. The reserve policemen faced choices, and most of them committed terrible deeds. But those who killed cannot be absolved by the notion that anyone in the same situation would have done as they did. For even among them, some refused to kill and others stopped killing (Browning 1998: 188).

And yet, while not deterministic, the causal patterns discussed in this chapter are probabilistic and thus contribute to explaining the patterns of cruelty and genocide.

> [For example,] ... the behavior of Police Battalion 101 has deeply disturbing implications. There are many societies afflicted by traditions of racism and caught in the siege mentality of war or threat of war. Everywhere society conditions people to respect and defer to authority, and indeed could scarcely function otherwise. Everywhere people seek career advancement. In every modern society, the complexity of modern life and the resulting bureaucratization and specialization attenuate the sense of personal responsibility of those implementing official policy. Within virtually every social collective, the peer group exerts tremendous pressure on behavior and sets moral norms. If the men of Police Battalion 101 could become killers under such circumstances, what group of men cannot? (Browning 1998: 188)

In conclusion, genocide scholarship points to a core set of explanatory factors. Some arguments correspond with criminological theory. Yet, criminologists have much work to do to successfully apply their theories to genocide and other gross HR crimes. Reading studies of genocide scholars should inspire criminologists—and they will eventually be able to pay back.

FIVE

how can criminology address contemporary atrocities?

First we will examine the case of Darfur, and how modern criminological data collection and analysis are advancing the understanding of genocide, especially in combination with a theory that takes collective action seriously. We then encounter the "dark side of organizations," a crucial theme as most gross human rights violations are committed through organizational actors—we apply this approach to the My Lai massacre. In each case, a description is followed by an attempt to explain and to offer general lessons for criminology.

How do criminologists investigate Darfur—and seek to explain it?

While almost all criminologists were silent on the gravest of crimes, John Hagan and his collaborators most recently sought to energetically put an end to such neglect. Following his work on the Balkan wars and the building of the International Criminal Tribunal for the former Yugoslavia (ICTY) in The Hague (Hagan 2003), Hagan has now engaged with the ongoing genocide in the Darfur region of Sudan (Hagan and Rymond-Richmond 2009). This new body of work provides us with an opportunity to lay out central elements of a current genocide and sketch ways in which criminologists may draw on different traditions to portray and explain this crime of crimes.

Beginning in the mid-1980s, the Darfur region of Sudan in Northern Africa ended a long period of peaceful coexistence, in which Arab herders and Black African farmers had engaged in economic exchange for their mutual benefit. In fact, few thought in terms of racial difference in Darfur during those happier days. Yet, peaceful co existence gave way to conflict and eventually to the ongoing genocide that so far has cost hundreds of thousands of lives, accompanied by tens of thousands of brutal rapes and millions of people displaced in concentration camps inside Sudan and refugee camps in the neighboring country of Chad.

Hagan and collaborators make use of a surprising empirical source, the Atrocities Documentation Survey (ADS), to describe and explain the genocide. The ADS is a rich data set gathered through a systematic survey of more than 1,100 Darfurians in the refugee camps in Chad, at the initiative of the US State Department under its Secretary Colin Powell in 2004. Based on this survey and supplemental data, the authors pieced together the unfolding of the deadly events in Darfur.

What occurred in Darfur?

In the mid-1980s, famine, associated with the desertification of the arid Sahel Zone south of the Sahara, produced ever more difficult living conditions for local populations. Challenges increased further for the local Black population when the national government under President al-Mahadi advanced a massive Arabization campaign that was intensified after a military coup by the new Sudanese president Omar al-Bashir. When the resulting pressure on the local Black population provoked some armed resistance by militant groups, the government responded with massive force. It armed local Arab militias, the so-called Janjaweed ("men on camels") and initiated a campaign of coordinated attacks on Black African villages. Often the Sudanese military bombs villages from the air, following up with joint ground attacks by Sudanese troops and Janjaweed. The targeting of attacks is specifically directed at Black tribal groups. Neighboring Arab settlements are spared. Attackers commonly shout racial epithets, and Black women and girls are brutally raped and gang-raped in the thousands. Here too the racial message is explicit: "We will kill all men and rape the women. We want to change the color" (quoted in Hagan and Rymond-Richmond 2009: 10). In addition to mass killings and mass rapes, massive expropriation takes place. Money, farm equipment, animals, and seed are taken, and huts are burned to the ground. In short, the economic basis of any survivors is systematically destroyed. The next step is displacement. Survivors are forced from their land into refugee camps in neighboring Chad and concentration camps in Sudan, partially overseen by Ahmad Harun, a government minister, who is charged by the ICC with crimes against humanity. The process, pursued with the greatest intensity in the most densely settled and most fertile areas, is completed with a resettlement of Arab groups into the emptied spaces in the Darfurian landscape.

Quotations from survivor interviews serve to illustrate the suffering and the racial implications:

> The village was attacked by the Antinovs, Migs, six helicopters … Vehicles and Janjaweed surrounded the village … Small trucks came with the Doskas (guns on top) … 30 men in each. Green uniforms. Leader had red stars on shoulders. Took 15 men away. Five girls taken, village burnt. Burned Mosque with minaret on top … [8] [A women reports:] A soldier took my baby son and said, "I will kill him." I told the soldier, "You killed my husband, don't kill my boy." … I was knocked down, and the first soldier had sex with me from the front. They were saying the government from Karthum sent [them] … Ten soldiers raped me and left me. I was bleeding and could not walk. They did this to me for nearly three hours [10] (quoted after Hagan and Rymond-Richmond 2009: 8–10).

The shouting of racial epithets was common during these attacks: "They called her Nuba [a derogatory term for Blacks], dogs, son of dogs, and we came here to kill you and your kids" (9).

Such reports of cruelty are backed up by a systematic statistical analysis of the ADS (see Map 1 on p. 71). The researchers were able to identify in which settlement cluster respondents had lived before they sought refuge in the camps of Chad. They also had information on the perpetrators and the acts, reports of persons killed, raped and abducted, and the shouting of racial epithets during the attacks, and on the density of settlements indicating fertility of the land. Circles in the map represent, by quartile, the proportion of victims hearing racial slurs. The numbers within the circles indicate the quartile ranking of a settlement cluster in terms of total victimization and of sexual victimization. The patterns in this map show what sophisticated statistical analyses confirm: greatest victimization occurs where the land is most fertile (southwest). Furthermore, total and sexual victimization are highest where attacks are most often accompanied by racial slurs. The expression of racial hatred thus appears to mobilize the attackers, to ignite a collective fury that encourages killing and raping and that is common in the context of genocidal action.

By the beginning of 2007, Luis Moreno-Ocampo, who had come to fame as a courageous prosecutor of Argentinian generals from the "Dirty War" era in his native country, and who is now chief prosecutor of the newly created ICC had completed two years of investigatory work into the atrocities of Darfur. In February 2007 he asked the ICC's Judicial Chamber to issue summons to two individuals, Sudanese government minister Ahmad Muhammad Harun and Ali Abd-Al-Rahman, an Arab militia leader, to appear before the court. The judicial chamber actually went further and issued warrants for their arrest. Moreno-Ocampo had alleged only crimes against humanity and war crimes, limiting consideration of race to a few descriptions of racial epithets in the attacks—he did not initially charge the accused with genocide. Yet, his theory of liability explicitly involved a group acting with a common purpose.

In response to such caution, Hagan and Rymond-Richmond engage in something previously unknown in criminology, but paralleled in the world of journalism by early twentieth century "muckrakers" such as Upton Sinclair. They first assemble evidence from the ADS interviews against the two suspects cited above and against additional individuals. Secondly, they document the group dynamics and collective action at work while simultaneously demonstrating the agency and initiative of liable individual actors. This criminological approach attempts to match the judicial construction of a "joint criminal enterprise," previously applied in the proceedings against former President Milošević at the ICTY in The Hague. It shows that individual liability exists in the context of collective action. Thirdly, Hagan and Rymond-Richmond seek to demonstrate that genocide was committed in addition to war crimes and crimes against humanity. Linking the criteria from the legal definition of genocide with the empirical evidence, they easily show that: members of a group are being killed and serious bodily and

Settlement Cluster Map of Racial Epithets and Total Victimization and Sexual Victimization

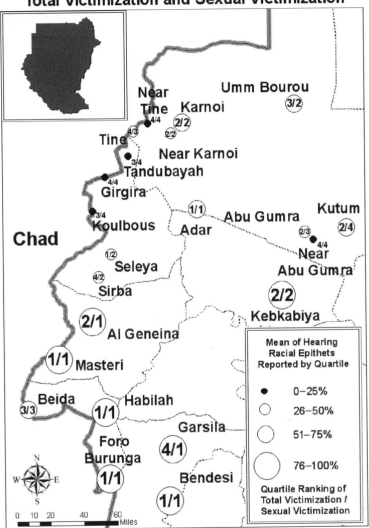

Map 1

Reprinted with permission from: John Hagan and Wenona Rymond-Richmond.
Darfur and the Crime of Genocide. Cambridge University Press, 2009.

mental harm is inflicted on them; and conditions of life are deliberately inflicted on them, calculated to bring about their physical destruction. Yet, the major challenge is the delivery of empirical proof of the intent to destroy, in whole or in part, a racial and ethnic group. To prove this point, Hagan and Rymond-Richmond make use of the impressive evidence regarding when and where racial epithets are used, and the links between such epithets and the intensity of killings and rapes (illustrated in Map 1). The authors thus achieve what has never been done in empirical scholarship: they mobilize its full potential to provide evidentiary proof of genocide.

Meanwhile, the justice process took additional steps. In July 2008, Moreno-Ocampo applied for an arrest warrant against Sudan's President Omar al-Bashir, charging him with genocide, crimes against humanity and war crimes. In March 2009, the ICC approved the arrest warrant for crimes against humanity and war crimes, but not for genocide. While the prosecutorial strategy was only partially successful, and despite the empirical evidence provided by Hagan and Rymond-Richmond, this is a historic moment as it is the first time a sitting president has been charged by the ICC.

How can criminology explain the genocide in Darfur?

Hagan and Rymond-Richmond (2009) not only document, they also seek to explain the genocide in Darfur, putting to use sociologist Ross Matsueda's (2006) model of a complex criminological theory that warrants a brief introduction here. Matsueda links the following building blocks that appear suited as a starting point toward a criminological genocide theory. He begins with:

1　Sutherland's expansion of his social psychological ideas about differential association toward differential organization to explain group-specific rates of criminal behavior through the balance of organization in favor of crime versus organization against crime.

2　Matsueda then strengthens Sutherland's social organization model by introducing network ideas. In social organization characterized by closed networks, interactions are restricted to similar others, intentions and meanings tend to be transparent, rigid norms govern behavior, speech patterns follow "restricted codes," which are context dependent and known among members of the in-group (e.g., Janjaweed, SS).

3 Matsueda further expands Sutherland's dynamic interpretation of "social organization" by introducing Meadian ideas: shared goals and division of labor emerge through social interaction, in line with earlier ideas by Peter Berger and Thomas Luckmann, and individual decisions are practical solutions to non-routine situations arrived at in interactive processes (remember Police Battalion 101 in Józefów, where police officers had to renegotiate through interaction, in radically new situations, what actions their proper role entailed).

4 Matsueda's next building block are Goffmanian framing ideas, specifically collective action frames (Benford and Snow 2000): "emergent beliefs and meanings that foster social movements by framing a problematic situation as calling for an action-oriented solution" (Matsueda 2006: 19). Such frames are especially effective if they define the root of the problem and its solution collectively ("we are all in this together"), the antagonists as "us" versus "them" (e.g., "Jews versus Aryans"; "Blacks versus Arabs"), and a problem or injustice caused by "them" that can be challenged by "us."

5 Closed and dense social networks with such collective action frames are most likely to produce collective efficacy, "the willingness … [of groups] to intervene for the common good" (Sampson and Raudenbush 1999: 919), accelerating collective action against or for crime.

6 Matsueda finally identifies the special role of actors who are central to local networks, but who also are linked to the outside world. They possess "social efficacy," an "ability to create consensus over group … objectives and procedures, and translate these procedures into action" (Matsueda 2006: 24). Capable of recognizing interests of their local group and of outside institutions and able to switch between local and universal codes, such actors may play crucial roles in manipulating local groups on behalf of collective goals, including a state's genocidal project.

Hagan and Rymond-Richmond link central elements of this model with James Coleman's (1990) famous micro-/macro-scheme and creatively apply this amalgam to explain the genocide in Darfur. At the macro-sociological level, resource competition results from the desertification of parts of the Darfur region. It combines with the Sudanese government's Arabization policies and supremacist ideologies directed against the Black African tribes. Organized "demonizing" creates and reinforces socially constructed Arab and Black identities, thus creating a collective action frame with the typical "us" versus "them" theme. As a result we find Black African groups, the Fur, Jebel, Masaleit and Zaghawa on one side of the constructed divide and Arab forces, the Janjaweed militias and Sudanese military on the other, combined with a "vocabulary of motive" in which "race" plays a central role. Such motivation feeds action at the micro-level where specific actors with high levels of "social efficacy" play crucial roles in establishing ideological and resource links between government and militias. Consider Musa Hilal, the son of an important Sheik among the increasingly impoverished Arab nomadic groups in North Darfur. The government had released Hilal from jail and sent him on a mission to establish links between the government and the Janjaweed. In his own words: "Our job is to mobilize people—the government has told us to mobilize people." Abdallah Gosh, head of the National Security and Intelligence Service confirms this mission: "[Hilal] was invited by the government to back the government Army, and he gave the people guns and leadership" (quoted after Hagan and Rymond-Richmond 2009: 123).

Crucial individuals such as Hilal, through their actions thus provide groups with military hardware and ideological tools. They feed into group processes, that are fueled by racial epithets and cursing and degrade the intended victims. The process thus aggregates back from the level of individual attitudes, motives and actions to the "collective racial intent," and further to systematic macro-social patterns of "ethnic cleansing," genocidal victimization, and eventually new settlement patterns.

In short, Hagan and Rymond-Richmond show how modern tools of criminological data collection and analysis can document patterns of genocide. In addition, by applying Matsueda's building blocks toward a complex criminological theory in combination with Coleman's famous micro-macro model to the Darfur data, they point the way toward an appropriate criminological genocide theory.

What role do formal organizations play in the execution of massacres? the case of My Lai

Grave human rights violations typically involve formal organizations such as military units or police departments. Our introductory cases of Argentina, South Africa, and the Balkans demonstrate this as much as the Shoah and the genocide of Darfur. While most genocidal actions discussed so far constitute standard operating procedure, organizational action also fares prominently in battlefield atrocities to which we now turn.

Our case here is the well known massacre executed by American soldiers in the hamlet of My Lai, village of Song My, in the northern part of South Vietnam during the Vietnam War. Events are described in a Pulitzer prize-awarded book by journalist Seymour Hersh (1970), entitled *My Lai 4* after the sub-hamlet where the major atrocities were committed, and the US Army's Peers Commission report, named after Lieutenant General W.R. Peers, who led an investigatory commission examining the events (Goldstein et al. 1976).

What occurred in My Lai?

According to the Peers Commission the following occurred:

> During the period 16–19 March 1968, US Army troops of TF [Task Force] Barker, 11th Brigade, American Division, massacred a large number of noncombatants in two villages of Son My Village, Quang Ngai Province, Republic of Vietnam. The precise number of Vietnamese killed cannot be determined but was at least 175 and may exceed 400. (2) The massacre occurred in conjunction with a combat operation which was intended to neutralize Son My Village as a logistical support base and staging area,

and to destroy elements of an enemy battalion thought to be located in the Son My area. (3) The massacre resulted primarily from the nature of the orders issued by persons in the chain of command within TF Barker ... (5) Prior to the incident, there had developed within certain elements of the 11th Brigade a permissive attitude toward the treatment and safeguarding of noncombatants which contributed to the mistreatment of such persons during the Son My operation. (6) The permissive attitude in the treatment of Vietnamese was, on 16–19 March 1968, exemplified by an almost total disregard for the lives and property of the civilian population of Son My Village on the part of commanders and key staff officers of TF Barker. (7) On 16 March, soldiers at the squad and platoon level, with some elements of TF Barker, murdered noncombatants while under the supervision and control of their immediate superiors. (8) A part of the crimes visited on the inhabitants of Son My Village included individual and group acts of murder, rape, sodomy, maiming, and assault of noncombatants and the mistreatment and killing of detainees. They further included the killing of livestock, destruction of crops, closing of wells, and the burning of dwellings in several subhamlets ... (19) At every command level within the American Division, actions were taken, both wittingly and unwittingly, which effectively suppressed information concerning the war crimes committed at Son My Village ... (Goldstein et al. 1976: 314–16).

The summary entails additional sections on the inadequacy of reports, investigations and reviews, of policies, directives and training, and on the actions of individuals involved in the massacre. The report only covers the period between 16 March 1968 and 29 March 1969, the date on which Ronald Ridenhour, a Vietnam veteran sent a letter to the president, Pentagon officials and members of the US Congress, in which he revealed information he had gathered on the massacre and its cover-up. Due to the secrecy of the Commission's work, Ridenhour believed that the cover-up was continuing. His subsequent contact with journalist Seymour Hersh resulted in Hersh's book, which drew massive public attention to the case. The journalistic account adds graphic detail to the Commission report:

The killings began without warning. ... There were few physical protests from the people; about eighty of them were taken quietly from their homes and herded together in a plaza area ... [First Platoon commander Lt.] Calley left [subordinates] Meadlo, Boyce and a few others with the responsibility of guarding the group. "You know what I want you to do with them," he told Meadlo. Ten minutes later—about 8:15A.M.—he returned and asked, "Haven't you got rid of them yet? I want them dead." Radioman Sledge who was trailing Calley, heard the officer tell Meadlo to "waste them." Meadlo followed orders: "We stood about ten to fifteen feet away from them and then he [Calley] started shooting them. Then he told me to start shooting them. I started to shoot them. So we went ahead and killed them ... Women were huddled against their children, vainly trying to save them ..." By this time there was shooting everywhere ... Brooks and his men in the second platoon to the north had begun to systematically ransack the hamlet and slaughter the people, kill the livestock and destroy the crops ... The men continued on, making sure no one was escaping. "We came to where the soldiers had collected fifteen or more Vietnamese men, women and children in a group ... [Captain and Company commander] Medina said: 'Kill every one. Leave no one standing'." A machine gunner began firing into the group. Moments later one of Medina's radio operators slowly "passed" among them and finished them off (Hersh 1970: 49–54).

How can formal organizations contribute to atrocities?

The My Lai massacre evolved from a battlefield mission. Company C had orders (and had expected) to fight a Vietcong Battalion in My Lai. Even though its men encountered only civilians, the massacre in which they engaged would be appropriately labeled a battlefield atrocity. Randall Collins (2008) recently developed a powerful micro-sociological argument to account for such deeds. He argues that humans do not easily engage in violence and cites stunning evidence from war time research according to which high percentages of soldiers, even in battle do not fire their weapons (43). The likelihood that they do depends on social interactions in specific contexts. Situations that produce violence are typically "shaped by an emotional field of tension and fear" (18), that are overcome when they are turned into emotional energy; and such energy drives violent action. Collins calls these reactions "forward panics," which are particularly frequent in the context of guerrilla warfare, where regular armies suffer most losses when they are not directly engaged in battle. Only their forward operations lead them into the "... danger zone, building up frustration and anticipation at finally reaching the enemy, and triggering moments when the enemy seems to have been caught; a frenzied rush of destruction" (88). The situation is further intensified in My Lai-type situations, when troops are brought into a landing zone by helicopter in the middle of enemy territory. Here "frenzied attacks of forward panic" become most likely, and military leadership placed American soldiers frequently in such situations during the Vietnam War. Massacres similar to that in My Lai—albeit not always with such high numbers of victims and rape campaigns—likely occurred in many unknown cases, as suggested by extensive quotes from a report by Marine Lt. Philip Caputo, a Vietnam Veteran (Collins 2008: 83–7; see also the 1972 documentary film *Winter Soldier*).

Situational context thus provokes violence, including battlefield atrocities. Yet, not all soldiers in Company C were equally engaged in the killings. Some did so only under duress when pushed by their superior officer, others refused. Also, the number of atrocities is likely to vary across divisions during the Vietnam War and across wars, including comparable wars with guerilla enemies. This leads us to questions about the organizational context in which situations are created that produce "forward panics," and in which the consequences of such panics are more or less deadly.

Here we benefit from the work of a scholar, who has greatly contributed to our understanding of the "dark side of organizations," the many instances of regular rule breaking behavior that is characteristic of life even in legitimate organizations. Sociologist Diane Vaughan (1999, 2002) stresses that members of organizations are always exposed to structural pressures resulting from competition and gaps between goals and legitimate means. They are likely to resort to the violation of laws, rules and regulations in order to meet organizational goals. Such rule violations become more likely as necessary structural features of organizations, such as hierarchy or specialized subunits, create "structural secrecy," meaning they provide settings intra-organizationally where risk of detection and sanctioning are minimized. In addition, organizational processes such as the "normalization of deviance" (i.e., acceptance of deviant behavior as normal) provide normative support for illegality, a pattern that has been documented in some of the white-collar crime literature cited above.

Applying these ideas to My Lai, we encounter a military unit that certainly constituted an organizational opportunity structure. Company C consisted of more than 150 soldiers, with a field operating strength of 120, under the command of Captain Ernest Medina. It was divided into three platoons, each with its own leader at the rank of Lieutenant and, within platoons, squads (for details see Goldstein et al. 1976: 80–2). It was embedded in a Task Force and a Division, with the potential for intelligence gathering, planning and back-up. This unit can achieve, what is regarded in war times as legitimate organizational goals: killing hostile forces and defeating enemy military units—in My Lai supposedly the 48th Viet Cong Battalion.

Yet, such organization simultaneously holds potential for deviance. Company C was organizationally (and spatially) separated from other units and hierarchy levels. Structural secrecy applied as its members could assume that their actions would not become known beyond the company level. Indeed, news of the massacre originally seems to have been confined at the Division level: according to the Peers Commission report, actions were taken at every command level within American Division, which effectively suppressed information concerning the war crimes. In fact, intense efforts at a cover-up only failed by chance because of veteran Ronald Ridenhour's unusual efforts. It is also unusual that the unit was accompanied by a photographer, Roland Haeberle, who would document much of the ordered mass execution of unarmed women and children—instead of the expected battle. Structural secrecy might well have worked, and we do not know in how many cases it did work during the Vietnam War and other wars; and, in the end, it partially benefited many squads within Charlie Company, whose "spontaneous atrocities" became known, but never supported by the kind of evidence that would tie particular individuals to specific crimes to allow for criminal convictions.

Like division of labor, hierarchy, while necessary for the functioning of modern organizations, simultaneously harbors potential for organizational failure and deviance. Rigid hierarchies do not allow for flexibility when unexpected conditions occur and when time for communication is limited, while too much autonomy granted to subordinate units allows for deviation from organizational goals and norms. Autonomy may result, for example, from missing or vague instructions. Crucial orders given in the My Lai case provide an example (Goldstein et al. 1976: 87). The mission was encouraged and approved, albeit not in any specific detail, by Major General Koster and by Colonel Oram Handerson, commanding officer of the 11th Brigade. Colonel Handerson had also, on the day before the attack, critiqued previous lack of aggressiveness. The mission was planned by Lieutenant Colonel Barker, commanding officer of the Task Force, and his staff. LTC Barker gave his orders at a March 15 briefing, the day before the massacre. Based on false intelligence, according to which only Viet Cong were expected at My Lai at the time of the attack, the defeat of the 48th Viet Cong Battalion was the declared purpose. While no written instructions were issued, all evidence suggests that Barker at least implicitly ordered the destruction of houses, livestock and other foodstuff. No instructions were seemingly given regarding the treatment of noncombatants should any be found in the village (Goldstein et al. 1976: 94). Captain Ernest Medina, commander of Company C was the recipient of these murky orders, and he passed them down the hierarchy to his men. Again, there is doubt about how exactly Medina worded his orders. Lieutenant Calley, leader of the first platoon later charged that Medina ordered the killing of noncombatants. Yet, doubts remain as Calley's memory supported his use of the defense of superior orders in his later court-martial. Calley's own orders to his men were also initially ambiguous. After gathering a large number of villagers, Calley left the scene with the words "you know what to do with [them]." Only when he returned did he specify "I want them dead" (Kelman and Hamilton in Ermann and Lundman 2002: 202).

The case illustrates how hierarchy separates lower from higher levels of authority and opens up room for structural secrecy. Vague orders give lower units discretion and provide additional room for deviance—while simultaneously protecting higher ranks from later sanctions. The nature of the orders, especially when accompanied by pleas for more aggressiveness, may also have been perceived as authorization to massacre. Such authorization is one of the conditions of a sanctioned massacre, defined as an "act of indiscriminate, ruthless, and often systematic mass violence, carried out by military and paramilitary personnel while engaged in officially sanctioned campaigns, the victims of which are defenseless and unresisting civilians, including old men, women, and children" (Kelman and Hamilton in Ermann and Lundman 2002: 210):

> Through authorization the situation becomes so defined that the individual is absolved of the responsibility to make personal moral choices …
> In the My Lai massacre, it is likely that the structure of the authority situation contributed to the massive violence … by conveying the message that acts of violence against Vietnamese villagers were *required*, as well as the message that such acts, even if not ordered, were *permitted* by the authorities in charge (Kelman and Hamilton in Ermann and Lundman 2002: 215).

The likelihood of deviance is further affected by organizational culture. In the case of My Lai the Peers Commission diagnosed a "… permissive attitude toward the treatment and safeguarding of noncombatants within certain elements of the 11th Brigade. The Commission finds an almost total disregard for the lives and property of the civilian population of Son My village on the part of commanders and key staff of TF Barker" (Goldstein et al. 1976: 314).

Finally, emotions in preparation for violence may be cultivated and enhanced by organizational rituals. Rituals create collective effervescence, an intense sense of shared emotion, and they direct group members' attention toward a common goal (Durkheim 2001). The preparation for the My Lai massacre illustrates this point:

> Charlie Company was spoiling for a fight, having been totally frustrated during its months in Vietnam—first by waiting for battles that never came, then by incompetent forays led by inexperienced leaders, and finally by mines and booby traps. In fact, the emotion-laden funeral of a sergeant killed by a booby trap was held on March 15, the day before My Lai. Captain Medina gave the orders for the next day's action at the close of that funeral. Many were in a mood for revenge (Kelman and Hamilton in Ermann and Lundman 2002: 198).

The Peers Commission quotes several men from Company C, Allen Joseph Boyce among them: "… we were all 'psyched' up because we wanted revenge for some of our fallen comrades that had been killed prior to the operation in the general area of 'Pinkville'" (Goldstein et al. 1976: 100). Emotions produced by organization-level rituals thus add to the emotional energy into which tension and fear are transformed in the situation of violence itself (Collins 2008).

In short, under conditions of structural secrecy, a deviant organizational culture, and ritually enhanced emotions, the action of My Lai turned into a sanctioned massacre. The "forward panic," already dangerous for the inhabitants of My Lai, became all the more deadly as a consequence of organizational arrangements and processes.

What role did the environment of formal organization play?

In addition to inner-organizational features, environmental uncertainty contributes to routine nonconformity, especially where uncertainty is coupled with the "liability of newness," a concept Vaughan (2002: 275) adopts from Art Stinchcombe. Both environmental uncertainty and newness were at work for Company C. Few soldiers were career soldiers; the majority were drafted, primarily from minority populations with relatively low levels of education. Military training was basic at best, knowledge about the local culture was neglected, and "... the handling and treatment of civilians or refugees was not covered ..." (Goldstein et al. 1976: 81). Further, the Company had arrived in Vietnam in December 1967, just four months before the massacre, and "a survey of the personnel assets of Company C indicates that none of the men had significant combat experience before the Son My operation and that this was their first major assault role" (Goldstein et al. 1976: 82). Finally, the soldiers were fighting a guerilla war, where the environment is always more uncertain than in traditional wars. Company C certainly acted under high levels of environmental uncertainty, and it was fraught with the liability of newness.

Further, the organizational environment includes definitions of the enemy as "commies" and "gooks," and both represented evil. Remember the hot phase of the Cold War between the US-led West and the Soviet Union-dominated Communist block. In South Vietnam the US was fighting North Vietnam and the Viet Cong, both of whom received massive material and logistic support from the Soviet Union. In addition, racist attitudes, reflected in the derogatory term "gooks," depicted the Vietnamese more as members of a category of people than as individuals, partially excluding them from the community of fellow humans. Under such circumstances inhibitions against killing, the product of a long civilizing process (Elias 1978), are most easily overcome. The appearance of the mistreated and their human misery finally confirms the dehumanizing image. It feeds into a vicious circle in which the risk of massacres is enhanced. In the words of Kelman and Hamilton, who highlight the "dehumanization" of victims of atrocities as one condition of sanctioned massacres: "Through dehumanization, the actors' attitudes toward the target and toward themselves become so structured that it is neither necessary nor possible for them to see the relationship in moral terms" (Kelman and Hamilton in Ermann and Lundman 2002: 215).

Individuals in organizations: action, cognition and meaning

Where do these accounts of organizations and their environment leave individual actors? Do they matter? The record of My Lai, like that of Police Battalion 101, indicates that they do. Even when exposed to the constraints, pressures and opportunities that organizations and their environment offer and impose, individual actors maintain agency. In My Lai, Pfc. Paul Meadlo initially did not act on Lieutenant Calley's vague order "You know what to do with them!" But when Calley later clarified "I want them dead!" and began to shoot, Meadlo followed suit—while crying; others appear to have simply obeyed. Pfc. James Joseph Dursi, however, refused successfully. Pfc. Herbert Carter incapacitated himself by self-inflicting a gun shot wound. Specialist Ronald Grzesik may even have confronted Calley. Finally, and most extraordinary, Hough Thompson, pilot of a reconnaissance helicopter landed between Calley's men and a group of victims. He had his crew turn its guns at their American comrades to put an end to the slaughter. Deviant within the immediate organizational context, such actions were consistent with international law, the military code of justice and norms assumed outside the situation and Company C.

Members of formal organizations and bureaucracies, including military units are thus not reduced to automatons. They do not live in an "iron cage" (Max Weber) with total loss of agency. When choosing their course of action, they may be helped by membership in multiple social circles (Georg Simmel) and their ability to transcend the current situation by envisioning a future with a normality that differs from that of their deviant peers (Giordano et al. 2002). And yet, Vaughan's organizational criminology shows how situational conditions, the weight of which Collins impressively demonstrates, may be embedded in, facilitated by, and produced by organizational context to produce atrocities.

Comparative notes and conclusions

A criminology of genocide and grave human rights violations is a project in progress. We already understand that the potential for grave human rights violations builds where:

1   Structural barriers affect groups or populations (Merton 1936) that

2   form oppositional cultures (Cohen 1955),

3   build social capital in the context of criminal organization (Sutherland 1947),

4   define movement frames in which they appear as victims and out-groups as evil (Benford and Snow 2000), and

5   thus establish collective efficacy (Sampson and Raudenbush 1999). These conditions apply to criminal gangs and genocidal groups alike.

6   The risk of genocide increases further when criminal regimes tap into (or grow out of) criminal movements (Hughes 1963) and

7   realign the balance of institutional power to advance their criminal purposes, consistent with our adaptation of Messner and Rosenfeld's (2007) institutional anomie argument.

8   Such regimes often create special groups for the execution of the dirtiest of work (e.g., Nazi SS; Janjaweed; but see Argentina's "Dirty War" where the entire military was involved),

9   foster and nourish them materially and ideologically, and equip them with means of violence (Hagan and Rymond-Richmond 2009), and

10 create situations that open up opportunities for violence, by instigating war or other forms of violence (Katz 1988; Brannigan and Hardwick 2003; Collins 2008).

11 Actors with high levels of "social efficacy" (Matsueda 2006) often play crucial roles, linking regimes and localized social groups and organizations with great potential for violence.

12 When regimes have substantial control-surplus (Tittle 1995), massive harm is predictable.

13 Control-surplus is inherent in the organizational apparatus of modern states (Vaughan 2002), especially where systems of checks and balances are missing.

In short, new insights on grave human rights violations are to be expected by drawing from different traditions within criminology. The previous chapter showed, in addition, how yet more can be gained from linking them with insights from scholars in genocide studies. Criminologists simultaneously expand the range of their theories, encounter additional rich substance and arrive at differentiations not previously achieved.

PART III
How can human rights violations be fought?

We answer this question in two steps. Chapter 6 reviews the types of courts that respond to human rights (HR) and humanitarian law (HL) violations. Then in Chapter 7 we examine the sociological conditions under which they function and the dilemmas and limits they face before we address their potential impact.

SIX

what is the role of criminal courts?

> The privilege of opening the first trial in history for crimes against the peace of the world imposes a great responsibility. The wrongs which we seek to condemn and punish have been so calculated, so malignant, and so devastating that humanity cannot tolerate their being ignored, because it cannot survive their being repeated. That four great nations, flushed with victory and stung with injury stay the hand of vengeance and voluntarily submit their captive enemies to the judgment of the law is one of the most significant tributes that Power has ever paid to Reason.

These are the famous sentences from the 22 November 1945 opening statement by US Supreme Court Justice Robert Jackson at the International Military Tribunal at Nuremberg (IMT). Jackson was the American chief prosecutor, and the trial was held against 22 leading members of the Nazi government and movement. "Staying the hand of vengeance" was no matter of course. Indeed, the idea of a trial with fair rules and due process protections had been in serious competition with alternative suggestions such as Stalinist show trials or summary executions of varying numbers of Germans. It also was revolutionary, to be put into practice for the first time in human history. The basis for the IMT had been laid by the August 1945 London agreement among the victorious powers. This was the serious beginning of the construction of international criminal courts as central institutions in the fight against grave humanitarian law (HL) and human rights (HR) violations.

How did international criminal courts emerge?

The occupying powers had arrested and Nuremberg's IMT had charged the defendants with crimes against the peace (conducting illegal, aggressive war), war crimes and crimes against humanity. The trial focused on offenses committed during the war, covered by international HL. It shied away from challenging the notion of national sovereignty by not charging pre-war offenses of the totalitarian Nazi regime against German citizens. After eleven months of trial the defendants were convicted. Twelve were executed, seven received prison terms, and three were acquitted (on related trials, including the famous "doctors'" and "lawyers' trials" see Heberer and Matthäus 2008).

The first *international criminal courts* grew out of military victory. While "power" did reserve space for (judicial) "reason," to use Justice Jackson's terms, power based on means of physical coercion certainly provided the backdrop of these judicial proceedings. It did visibly what force always does: it backs up legitimate state action (Weber 1976).

The post-World War II movement toward international criminal justice seemed to come to a premature end right after its start. The Cold War, beginning in the late 1940s, produced intense rivalry between the US-led West and the Soviet Union-dominated East. Each side fiercely defended its respective hemisphere, often resorting to the use of blunt force with little regard for HL and HR. US interventions in Latin American countries such as Nicaragua or Chile, covered by the Monroe Doctrine, and the Soviet-led invasion in Hungary and Czechoslovakia provide stark examples. Four decades of Cold War offered little chance for international agreements on institutions under which political perpetrators against HR and HL could be tried (Turk 1982).

Only the breakdown of the Soviet Union and the end of the Cold War allowed for new initiatives; different from Nuremberg or Tokyo, they did not grow out of military victory. Instead, the UN Security Council established both the ICTY in 1993 and the ICTR in 1994; and an international agreement, the Rome Statute of 1998 created the ICC, the first permanent international criminal court. The Rome Statute entered into force in 2002 when 60 countries had ratified. As of 2008 there were only 108 ratifications, with several powerful members of the international community strongly opposed, including the US (see Fichtelberg 2008: 48–52).

While this chapter focuses on international courts, alternatives and supplements must be mentioned. First, *hybrid courts* emerged from agreements between the UN and national governments. These courts are staffed with groups of domestic and international judges applying domestic and international law. Recent examples include courts in Sierra Leone, East Timor, Kosovo, and Cambodia, the latter in a much delayed response to the genocidal mass killings of the 1970s under the Khmer Rouge regime. Such trials, typically conducted in the countries where the crimes were perpetrated, allow for easier access to victims and witnesses, while international participation may reduce the risk of partisan abuses of trials as revenge mechanisms by post-transition regimes—or, in the alternative, obstruction by past perpetrators who managed to hold on to political power under the new regime.

Second, foreign and domestic courts contribute to international criminal justice. *Foreign courts* became famous through the Jerusalem trial against Adolf Eichmann (Arendt 1964). More recently a Spanish judge charged Chilean General Pinochet and (unsuccessfully) requested his extradition from the U.K. Cases tried in foreign courts remain rare though while *domestic courts* are a prominent part of international justice when they apply international HL and HR law, often in combination with domestic law. Importantly, domestic courts now operate under the shadow of the ICC. Its mere existence is likely to encourage domestic enforcement as most countries prefer cases to be handled at the domestic level (Sikkink 2009). Crucial here is the ICC doctrine of complementarity—it can only take up cases if domestic courts are unable or unwilling to do so. Domestic courts, however, tend to try top leaders only after regime changes (e.g., Argentina, Chile, Iraq), while low-level defendants are targeted in cases of regime continuity. Examples are the cases of My Lai and abuse and torture in the Abu Ghraib or Guantánamo Bay prisons (on commander-in-chief liability see Stewart 2006). In addition, penalties in these cases tended to be either mild or greatly reduced after initial sentencing.

How do international criminal courts work? the case of the ICTY

Formal Security Council decisions or international treaties are only the first and necessary steps toward creating international courts. Their actual functioning depends on multiple social actors and forces, for which Hagan's work on the ICTY provides profound insights (Hagan 2003; Hagan and Levi 2005). Based on extensive interviews, years of ICTY court room observation and theoretical ideas by French sociologist Pierre Bourdieu (1987), Hagan identifies innovative actors in the judicial field, all with different strengths (or forms of capital) and exposure to various national legal traditions. These actors compete against and cooperate with others inside the court and in the world of diplomacy and international politics to bring their project to fruition. Success is never guaranteed.

The history of the ICTY began with intense competition between diplomats who sought to broker peace deals with leading actors in the Balkan wars on the one hand and human rights groups on the other. Rights groups, linked together in TANs (Chapter 2), pressed for the detention of those they deemed guilty of mass murders, mass rapes and ethnic cleansing, even while diplomats sought to negotiate with targets of these efforts over agreements to end the cruelties. Exposed to such competing actors, the UN Security Council eventually passed Resolution 780 in October 1992, creating a "Commission of Experts" to investigate the ongoing atrocities in the Balkans. The Commission's highly deter-mined second chair, Cherif Bassiouni, greatly advanced the chances of a Tribunal. Bassiouni garnered substantial support to build a documenta-tion center with evidence on 6,000 cases of war crimes in the Balkans. His evidence allowed for the establishment of "command responsibil-ity" of several Bosnian-Serb generals involved in years of terrorizing the civilian population of Bosnia's capital Sarajevo (host of the 1984 Winter Olympics) through regular shelling and sniper fire from the surrounding mountains. By spring 1994, Bassiouni was able to submit a final report and ship a container with 65,000 pages of documents and 300 hours of tapes with crucial evidence to The Hague.

Meanwhile, the UN Security Council had established the ICTY and appointed as chief prosecutor Richard Goldstone, a South African judge with impeccable human rights credentials but little criminal law experience. Goldstone, beginning his ICTY work with almost no funds, used his international contacts and continued media presence, to secure a $30 million budget. Yet, prosecutorial efforts were initially limited to the case of Duško Tadić, a low ranking defendant accused of numerous killings and rapes in the concentration camps of Bosnia. A massive budget encountered an almost empty court.

Subsequently, the testimony of Drazen Erdemović (see Introduction) provided crucial evidence on the genocidal killing of Srebrenica, allowing for additional indictments. Further evidence was produced when Goldstone's diplomatic contacts secured access to CIA aerial images of mass graves around Srebrenica, allowing ICTY investigators to advance their massive exhumation project. Still, after two years and 70 indictments, only six suspects were in custody. Desperate, the court had resorted to legally problematic "in absentia" hearings against defendants who were not in the custody of the court.

This situation greeted Canadian jurist Louise Arbour, Goldstone's successor, when she took over the position of Chief Prosecutor in 1996. Arbour had substantial expertise in criminal law and sought to transform the "virtual tribunal" with its questionable "in absentia" hearings into a "real time tribunal" (Hagan 2003: 93–131). She linked traditional tools of criminal law with the UN mandate by introducing sealed (secret) indictments and surprise arrests, through NATO military forces. As a result, 30 people were in custody by June 1998. Arbour also successfully pressured several governments to tie financial aid to Balkan countries to their cooperation with the ICTY. While her attempt to enter Kosovo to investigate allegations of genocide during the Kosovo war failed, media reporting of the event dramatized the situation and allowed investigators to enter Kosovo together with the troops once NATO intervened militarily.

Such success provided crucial evidence to Carla Del Ponte, former Swiss Attorney General, who succeeded Arbour as Chief Prosecutor in 1999. Based on this evidence, Del Ponte convinced Western governments to exert financial pressure on Serbia to extradite former president Slobodan Milošević. Documenting the occurrence of widespread, systematic attacks on civilians, including the rape campaigns of Foca, Del Ponte proved that crimes against humanity had been committed. She introduced, against challenges by the presiding judge, intercept telephone evidence of General Krstić (see Introduction), ordering a subordinate: "... kill them all. God dam it ... [Not a] single one must be left alive" (quoted after Hagan and Levi 2005: 1521). She was finally able to charge former President Milošević with genocide in the Kosovo case where his position in the chain of command was clearer than in the Bosnian civil war, and where the evidence was fresher. Throughout, innovative strategies—at times merging common law and continental civil law traditions—became *doxa*, new taken for granted legal standards in the emerging international criminal tribunal in The Hague.

In short, Hagan's account of the ICTY illustrates that Security Council resolutions alone do not determine the fate of a newly founded international criminal court. Innovative strategies, involving cooperating and competing legal actors, but also actors from the worlds of diplomacy and military, from national governments, IGOs and NGOs, unfold in the face of uncertain outcomes before a new type of international criminal legal practice can be established.

Do institutional incentives and constraints matter? the case of the ICC

Once institutions are established, their shape impacts ideas, practices and outcomes. Recent comparative studies on punishment have shown, for example, that elected prosecutors and judges tend to be more receptive to moral panics than their life-tenured civil service colleagues in other countries (Savelsberg 1994; Sutton 2000). We should thus look more closely at the organization of the ICC, the first permanent international criminal court. The court's structure, determined by the Treaty of Rome, consists of several courts or "chambers" with a total of 18 judges, each with non-renewable nine-year terms (for details see Schabas 2007). Trial and appeals chambers write opinions and thus specify future international criminal law. The prosecutor, currently the Argentinean Luis Moreno-Ocampo, is also selected for one non-renewable nine-year term through an anonymous vote of the member states. Cases can be referred to the ICC prosecutor by individual citizens of member states, by states (including non-member states) against one of their citizens, and by the UN Security Council. The latter, for example, referred the Darfur case to the ICC;

cases against Uganda, the Central African Republic and the Democratic Republic of Congo were referred to the ICC by state parties (http://www.icc-cpi.int/cases.html).

What are we to expect from the ICC in light of this institutional setup? The court will certainly not be as activist and punitive as American criminal courts have been in recent decades. This is first due to the principle of complementarity: as opposed to the ICTY which had supremacy over domestic jurisdiction—the ICC can only get involved with Security Council referral or if domestic courts are unable or unwilling to prosecute. Second, given the relatively weak institutionalization of civil society at the world level, moral outrage is less likely to be a factor than at the national level. Third, even in cases of moral outrage, prosecutors and judges, holding tenured and non-renewable positions, are less likely to give in to such pressure. Yet, civil rights NGOs and TANs may mobilize states or individuals. In the case of Darfur, public mobilization is likely to have advanced the Security Council's action. Further, given the strong role of nation states among the court's constituents, the court will often compete with diplomatic or military actors and outcome-oriented, rather than procedural justice-oriented, reasoning. Finally, massive power-asymmetries between states are likely to be reflected in the court's agenda. The US, for example, has entered "Bilateral Immunity Agreements" with some 100 governments that agree not to extradite American citizens to the ICC, often in exchange for international aid. It is obvious that poor countries do not have such leverage.

Limited versus expanded jurisdiction? more on the ICC

The ICC's jurisdiction includes only four crimes: genocide, crimes against humanity, war crimes and aggression, committed after April 2002 in states that have ratified the Rome Treaty. Such limitations, in combination with the complementarity principle, helped secure the necessary number of signatories to the Rome Treaty. States still only hesitantly support a model that weakens state sovereignty.

Not surprisingly, HR advocates would like to extend substantially jurisdiction of the ICC or other criminal courts to include violations of all rights guaranteed in the UDHR. Sociologist Judith Blau and jurist Alberto Moncada (2007) suggest that child poverty in a wealthy country, for example, could be conceived of as an offense against the Convention for the Rights of the Child. Responsible states ought to be "punished through economic sanctions and through isolation in the world community" (2007: 371). These scholar-activists further propose extending individual criminal liability to those whose policies have advanced violations of international human rights standards (e.g., child labor prohibitions).

Yet, unsatisfactory as current limitations to HR jurisdiction may be, even proponents of expanded international criminal law see reasons to challenge such broad jurisdiction (e.g., Hagan and Levi 2007; Cerulo 2007). First, tort law may in many cases be at least as effective as criminal law, with lower burdens of proof; and alternative mechanisms such as truth commissions and reparation programs should also be considered. Second, charging countries and their leaders in criminal court may isolate these countries (and their allies) from the international community, polarizing conflict, and resulting in a loss of international influence altogether. Third, criminal law is ill-suited to address larger structural and cultural forces that contribute to HR violations. Fourth, the use of force in international relations is always problematic (see the US-led war against Iraq). Fifth, HR problems such as large-scale homelessness among children may result from national policies enacted by legitimate governments and backed by majorities of the electorate. Who then is to be charged? Finally, HR violations may result not from domestic policies but from supra-national processes such as international competition for capital or conditions imposed by IGOs.

Obviously, the path toward a system that advances HR by balancing criminal law with other types of law and with alternative non-legal interventions (and the principle of national sovereignty with legitimate interests of the international community in intervening) is thorny. Criminal law will be a necessary and helpful tool, but its reach will be limited.

Individual versus collective accountability?

While individual agency is always involved in cases of grave HR and HL violations, recent criminological research has documented how individual action is embedded in collective action (see the "collective criminal intent" in Darfur and organizational responsibility in the My Lai massacre). Interestingly, criminal law and justice have also increasingly addressed the notion of collective criminal actors, despite their traditional focus on individuals (Coleman 1990). How then does criminal law respond to collective actors, where there is "no soul to dam, no body to kick" (Coffee 1981)?

First is the concept of conspiracy, rooted in US jurisprudence and earlier common law traditions that increasingly made its way into international law. The crime of conspiracy is defined as an agreement between two or more individuals, entered into for the purpose of committing an unlawful act. It is justified as a separate crime as it is conceived of as a threat to the public in itself. Conspiracy encourages and eases criminal behavior, while the law seeks to deter (by increasing the cost of membership) and to destabilize (by undermining trust among co-conspirators) (on US legal models, for example in the RICO act, see Meierhenrich 2006: 345).

In international criminal law, Article 9 of the London Charter makes membership in a "criminal organization" punishable. Justice Jackson as chief prosecutor used this position when he argued that criminal organizations will serve as carriers of criminal plans from one generation to the next if not delegitimized by criminal law. "Conspiracy" made its next international appearance, albeit in a modified form, at the ICTY under the name of "joint criminal enterprise." Crimes that must be expected in the context of a joint criminal enterprise constitute individual criminal liability even if charged individuals are not themselves engaged in the execution of the crime. A person's involvement in the planning of ethnic cleansing campaigns to be conducted by armed groups, for example, should then result in charges of homicide and war crimes, as such campaigns must be expected to result in the killing of civilians.

And yet, "conspiracy," "criminal organizations," and "joint criminal enterprise," innovative attempts at resolving the legal dilemma of individual guilt in the context of collective action, face grave challenges. Especially, they raise the specter of guilt by association, thereby endangering the *nullum crimen sine lege* principle, and they thus create doubts regarding the rigor and impartiality of international criminal law.

A second innovation from American criminal law that also seeks to tackle the dilemmas posed by collective criminal action has not yet made its way into international criminal law. I mean the imposition of probationary conditions and penalties through the US corporate sentencing guidelines (Lofquist 1993). Passed in 1991, these guidelines pursue diverse goals: ensure satisfaction of other sanctions; impose effective prevention; reduce recidivism; and ensure organizational change if necessary to accomplish one of the traditional goals of sentencing (retribution, deterrence, incapacitation, rehabilitation). Mandatory conditions of probation include: commission of no further crime and the payment of fines, restitution, and/or performance of community service. Should a corporation be unable to pay fines, the court may oversee its activities for up to five years (e.g., impose duties to report finances, submit to unannounced audits). Discretionary conditions of probation may include: media publicity, prevention plans, notifying employees and shareholders, progress reports to the court, and the examination of facilities by the court. Such innovative methods have made a dent into the individualistic limits of American criminal law. They also reach beyond a simplistic market logic (e.g., deterrence through fines) to take seriously organizational theory, the recognition that crime is rooted in the structure of organizations (Etzioni 1993).

Does the case of corporate sentencing guidelines entail lessons for international criminal justice? Several challenges would have to be met. First is the enforcement of court orders if a hostile regime refuses to obey, a problem long faced by UN Treaty bodies. Second, in case of grave atrocities, a negotiated settlement with the perpetrating collectivities is often inconceivable and may undermine the legitimacy of the court. Dissolution of corporate entities and punishment of their individual members are typically called for (see Iraqi Republican Guards; Nazi SS). Third, collective punishment disregards considerable shades of culpability if the collectivity is defined too inclusively. Fourth, collective punishment may open collectivities up to the lure of oppositional cultures, if it is directed against large populations or entire countries. The punishment of Germany after World War I served as a warning to the victors of World War II. They sought to penalize relatively small groups of leading Nazis while simultaneously introducing the Marshall Plan to help the majority of Germans out of post-war desolation. While this strategy had problematic side effects, it helped lay the foundation for the first stable democracy in German history.

Political reason versus procedural fairness?

An underlying tension in criminal justice has been between a strict formal or procedural application of rules versus an orientation toward practical outcomes (Savelsberg 1992). The former orientation is typically offense-oriented, associated with determinate sentencing law, where specific crimes (plus previous convictions) determine the punishment. The latter model takes offenders and their circumstances into consideration. It is associated with indeterminate law where expected outcomes guide the court's decision. What will the sentence mean, for example, for future reintegration into a law-abiding life, what for the convict's dependents or employees? In our case, how will it impact the transition from war to peace or from dictatorship to democracy?

Given the high stakes of trials against serious HL and HR violators, the practical consequences of a court's rulings must play a crucial role. Justice Jackson had argued that failure to legally denounce the organizations involved in the Nazi crimes would open the doors to a recurrence of massive genocide in the next generation, and that humankind would not survive a repeat of such horrors. How could the IMT, the ICTY, or the ICC then not be mindful of the substantive consequences of their proceedings? How could any of them stick to formal rules on their own?

And yet, some legal philosophers argue that formal principles, a "just desert" orientation and a focus on rights of the accused must trump policy in international criminal justice (Fichtelberg 2006). Even the IMT has come under liberal attack for its breach of formal rules, despite general agreement regarding its relative success in producing justice. Landsman (2005: xi), a self-described "American trial lawyer, legal academic, and Jew," for example, critiques the IMT's breach of liberal legal principles, such as the admission of hearsay evidence. Such philosophical arguments are backed by the conviction that only strictly due process-oriented international criminal justice can earn legitimacy and that only a legitimate system can prevail in the long term.

In conclusion, domestic, hybrid, foreign and international courts have become increasingly involved in HR matters. International courts or tribunals, once created, require resourceful actors with different types of capital, to successfully fight challengers and to actually get a functioning court off the ground. The specific institutional forms courts take have massive implications for how they function. Finally, courts involved in HR issues, even more than other courts, face diverse fields of tension: between formal-procedural versus pragmatic outcome orientation, restricted versus expanded jurisdiction, and individual versus collective accountability.

SEVEN

how effective can courts be and what can help them?

In the final chapter, we consider criminal law's potential impact by way of (a) deterrence and (b) the delegitimization of offenses via the construction of collective memories of evil. Recognizing both, potential and limitations, we then examine alternative and supplemental institutions such as Truth Commissions that may overcome some of the limits of criminal courts in the fight against humanitarian law (HL) and human rights (HR) violations.

Many forces are at work when regimes and their agents engage in gross violations of HL and HR law. For genocide, historians and political scientists identified explanatory factors such as war, totalitarianism, societal crises, ideological mobilization, and racism or anti-Semitism. Obviously, given the broad nature of the contributing factors, crime control policies alone cannot prevent evil. Constitutional frames and practices, regulating the distribution of societal and state power, fiscal and trade policies, diplomacy and military intervention, welfare and education programs, infrastructure and media all contribute to conditions under which humanitarian and HR crimes become more or less likely and consequential. But crime control may yet play a crucial supplementary role.

Are criminal courts effective?

As in other cases of penal intervention against the mighty, we find typical patterns reversed: conservatives are the skeptics and liberals the optimists (Savelsberg with Brühl 1994). Conservative critics include Goldsmith and Krasner (2003), the former a University of Chicago law professor who worked for the Pentagon during the G.W. Bush administration.

Goldsmith and Krasner first mistrust the rise of universal jurisdiction, the power of domestic courts to try foreign citizens, summarized in the Princeton Principles of Universal Jurisdiction and justified by the recognition that human rights violations are offenses to all humanity (http://www1.umn.edu/humanrts/instree/princeton.html). Domestic courts, they argue, may have little sense of the harm their prosecutions may cause in the affected foreign country. Amnesties, truth commissions and other transitional justice programs, and thus successful transitions to peace and democracy may be at risk.

The ICC is a second target of critique. The court, Goldsmith and Krasner argue, is marred by vague norms. And, like universal jurisdiction, it suppresses the consideration of power, necessary to assess the consequences of intervention and to balance legal accountability with political costs. They argue that filing charges against Serb President Milošević by the prosecutors of the ICTY, for example, made it impossible for NATO to reach a deal with Serbia, thereby extending war and suffering in the Balkans in the summer of 1999. Today these critics would challenge the ICC for its decision to charge Sudanese President al-Bashir with genocide, at a time where his role in reaching a peace deal for the enduring bloody conflict in Southern Sudan may be crucial. In general, the concern is that perpetrators will not be willing to negotiate and give up power if they are threatened by criminal trials (also Snyder and Vinjamuri 2003/2004).

On the other side of the debate are the optimists, prominent among them political scientist Kathryn Sikkink. Sikkink challenges the skeptics with an impressive new data set with information on domestic truth commissions and domestic, foreign and international trials for a 26-year period (1979–2004), covering 192 countries and territories. Her analyses shows the following (Sikkink and Booth-Walling 2007): of all the countries 34 instated truth commissions and 49 transitional trials in response to HR abuses such as summary executions, disappearances, torture, arbitrary arrest and imprisonment. More than two thirds of transitional and new countries used some mechanisms, and over half applied some form of judicial proceeding. Against widely held beliefs, transitional justice continues long after transitions. Countries often begin with truth commissions that frequently are followed by trials, sometimes with much delay and despite assurances of amnesty. Statistical analyses indicate first, against the skeptics, that transitional justice does not typically lead to strengthening of old forces; the severity of offences and likelihood of trials are highly correlated (decisions for trials are thus not made lightly); and, importantly, countries with more human rights trials showed greater improvements of later human rights records. Specifically, countries with truth commissions and trials had an improvement of 0.7 on the five point scale on which their human rights record was measured. Countries with trials alone had an improvement of 0.1, lower but still significant. Brazil, a country with minimal transitional justice intervention after its military dictatorship, showed a democracy score equal to those of the more interventionist countries of Argentina, Peru, Mexico, and El Salvador; yet, it fared far worse on a political terror scale. Importantly, and against the skeptics, not a single case in Latin America shows that holding a trial contributed to conflict and dislodged the transition.

The optimistic and skeptical positions are not necessarily mutually exclusive. Future research will have to examine in which contexts what kinds of interventions produce what consequences. Such research may well support the optimistic position and thus strengthen, from a social science perspective, institutions such as the ICC. Yet, it may also suggest modifications. Philosopher Max Pensky (2008), for example, suggests that the prosecutor of the ICC, following his mission, may indeed disregard a constellation of power that will extend suffering as a consequence of intervention. Drawing lessons from the case of Uganda, he argues that some mechanism of checks and balances should be in place to stop prosecutions if the political and humanitarian price to be paid for justice is too high. The price, of course, would be a less than independent judiciary.

How can we explain the correlation between transitional justice and better human rights outcomes identified by Sikkink? Could a third factor be at work, such as the establishment of the rule of law in a country's past, or does the correlation really represent a causal link between transitional justice and positive human rights records? If causality is involved, how does it work?

Rational actors or collective memories: what's in the black box?

Any argument based on single cases or even on quantitative data sets on a larger number of historical events has to contend with multiple confounding factors that cannot empirically be controlled for. Theoretical efforts toward understanding the link between trials and outcomes are thus crucial. They require us to open up the "black box" between intervention and human rights. Two processes may be at work. One is a deterrence mechanism, consistent with rational choice ideas; the other is a cultural mechanism, a thorough delegitimization of gross human rights abuses, possibly to the point where they no longer appear as options in the decision trees of rational actors. Such delegitimization may result from an appropriately constructed collective memory.

Rational choice ideas and deterrence research have a long tradition in criminology. One common conclusion of many studies is that the certainty of punishment is most likely to have a deterrent effect, more than its severity (Matsueda et al. 2006). White-collar crime literature suggests that deterrence is most likely to work for the powerful, as they are expected to act rationally. Sikkink's explanation of the positive correlation between transitional justice mechanisms and human rights records is consistent with this mode of thought: the next generation of military officers will remember the shaming their predecessors experienced as a result of criminal sanctions or truth commission reports and be reluctant to breach HR (Sikkink and Kim 2010). Simultaneously we recognize, however, that many perpetrators of the gravest violations were so radicalized, certainly distinct from corporate executives, that even the risk of death would not have deterred them from their murderous paths. I thus turn toward a cultural argument about the conditions under which horrors of the past are remembered in ways that thoroughly delegitimize past regimes and their atrocities. Even sophisticated rational choice arguments take learning about the past seriously, as such learning will affect what costs and benefits decision makers take into consideration (Matsueda et al. 2006).

Here a new line of academic work comes to play that examines the effects of trials and other mechanisms on collective memory (Osiel 1997; Savelsberg and King 2007, 2011). This work builds on classic sociological ideas and on arguments made by politicians and jurists such as President Franklin Roosevelt and Justice Robert Jackson. Consider Roosevelt's argument in favor of a criminal trial against the Nazi perpetrators. Judge Samuel Rosenman, Roosevelt's confidant reports about the president: "He was determined that the question of Hitler's guilt—and the guilt of his gangsters—must not be left open to future debate. The whole nauseating matter should be spread out on a permanent record under oath by witnesses and with all the written documents" (after Landsman 2005: 6). Here a new idea is added to the traditional rationales for criminal trials and sanctions such as retribution, deterrence or incapacitation: a history writing function, the construction of a collective memory of past evil that will reduce the likelihood of future offending.

Collective memory, a term coined in the classic work of French sociologist Maurice Halbwachs (1992), refers to knowledge about the past that is shared, mutually acknowledged and reinforced by a collectivity. Applied to horrendous events, we speak of cultural trauma, "a memory accepted and publicly given credence by a relevant membership group and evoking an event or situation that is a) laden with negative affect, b) represented as indelible, and c) regarded as threatening a society's existence or violating one or more of its cultural presuppositions" (Smelser in Alexander et al. 2004: 44).

Classical and contemporary research has long addressed the affective and cognitive functions of trials. Trials have been understood as "degradation ceremonies," leading to the ritual destruction of the accused and of any glorified collective memories peoples hold of former charismatic dictators (Garfinkel 1956). Other classical thinkers have similarly stressed the emotional aspects of trials that contribute simultaneously to "respect for the law" and "hatred for the criminal aggressor" (George Herbert Mead) and that help social sentiments maintain their force and vitality (Emile Durkheim). Applying such ideas to the issues at hand, Carlos Santiago Nino (1996), Argentinean jurist and former advisor to

President Raúl Alfonsín, argued that the prosecution of the Argentinean military junta was necessary to impress on the collective conscience that the law is the ultimate force in society. Anthropologist John Borneman (1997) took a similar position regarding Eastern Europe after the overthrow of Communist regimes.

Legal scholar Mark Osiel (1997), writing specifically about the role of law in the construction of collective memories of mass atrocities, both supports and challenges the positions taken by such Durkheimian protagonists of criminal trials. He stresses the importance of trials as places in which the "poetics" of story telling bear out, with defense attorneys telling the story as a tragedy and prosecutors as a morality play. To him, the court room drama is recast "in terms of the "theatre of ideas," where large questions of collective memory and even national identity are engaged" (Osiel 1997: 3). Osiel suggests "liberal show trials" conducted by "moral entrepreneurs" and, quoting Tzvetan Todorov, by "activists of memory." Yet, Osiel also claims that Durkheimians overlooked the role of reason and dissenting opinions (i.e., conflict) in court trials. In addition to their emotional function, trials may thus simultaneously provide a civil arena in which dissenting actors can tell their stories and have to listen to each other, thus contributing to solidarity through civil dissent and providing an institutional arena for the practice of communicative action. Osiel quotes John Dewey's dictum that "democracy begins in conversation" (1997: 45).

The hope invested in criminal trials and their contribution to history writing and to the formation of collective memory, however, must be cautioned. Trials follow a particular logic. Evidentiary rules differ, for example, from those used by historians. Further, trials target individuals, not the social processes and cultural patterns sociologists might focus on when constructing the past. Actions trials address are further limited by legal classification systems; producers of inflammatory rhetoric may have played central roles, but they will not be criminally liable (the recent conviction of a musician for inciting genocide in Rwanda was a great exception). Trials also focus on defendants. The voices of victims are heard only when they serve the court (on the ICTY see Stover 2005). Finally, following the binary logic of criminal law, the defendant is guilty or not guilty, a gross simplification by psychological standards.

A budding literature has thus begun to critically explore the consequences of trials for collective memory. Giesen (2004), for example, argues that German criminal trials against former Nazis served a "decoupling" function. In light of such trials, the German people could take the position of the third party, while individual guilt was assigned to a few in the court of law. As individual perpetrators were ritually expelled, the majority of Germans were offered a chance to avoid acceptance of collective guilt. Osiel (1997) applies this insight to French history. President Charles de Gaulle urged that post-World War II trials were directed against a few elite actors of the Vichy regime that had collaborated with the Nazis. Here too decoupling succeeded. By attaching guilt to some individuals through legal rituals, memory could be cleansed of the collaboration of many, and attention could be redirected from questions about their past to the reconstruction of France following war and occupation.

Just like the legal process was affected by political will in the French case, so were the Allied trials against German perpetrators (Landsman 2005: 111 for the IMT). The Allies decided to focus on just a few major Nazi perpetrators, as prosecuting all who had become guilty might have destabilized the country and its budding democracy, with additional counterproductive effects at the onset of the Cold War. This focus on few perpetrators, however, helped shape a view of history that saw the majority of Germans as victims of a small elite, thus repressing the memory of support and collaboration many had provided (Marrus in Heberer and Matthäus 2008).

What the above cases, against high-level perpetrators, have in common is that the trials followed conquest and/or regime change. Trials may construct very different collective memories though when past evil is processed in the context of regime continuity. The trial against perpetrators of My Lai, for example, where criminal guilt was attributed only to one low-ranked military, has contributed to the exculpation, not just of broader segments of the population, but also of political and military leadership in public memory. History textbooks used in American high schools may be one mediating factor. Research shows that most textbooks do not mention the My Lai case. Those that do, tend to present the massacre in line with the outcome of the trial, focusing on the deeds of Lt. Calley, but silencing the role played by higher ranks and the attempted cover up of the massacre (Savelsberg and King 2011).

Such processing of past atrocities may have advanced uncritical attitudes toward the institution of the military (*GSS News*, Number 20, July 2006) and contributed to a willingness by American military in current conflicts to offend against norms of HL (Mental Health Advisory Team 2006). The judicial handling of recent torture and illegal imprisonment cases is likely to further advance such attitudes.

Despite such misgivings, criminal justice mechanisms may still affect collective memory in ways that make future evil less likely. First, the delegitimization of past perpetrators may be crucial in transitions. Second, the selectivities of legal logic must not be overrated. After all, legal trials initiate the collection of evidence. While not all may be admitted in the court of law, such evidence nevertheless may be available to future historians, or it may be directly communicated to the public through mass media. Hagan (2003) documents the diversity of extralegal expertise of forensic scientists, victim workers, journalists and social scientists, mobilized by the ICTY to uncover forensic and interview-based empirical evidence of the atrocities committed during the Balkan wars. News of recently opened mass graves and liberated concentration camps reached a broad public through journalistic reports, independent of the success of translating these materials into evidence in the court's proceedings. Investigatory evidence may also be used in future historical documentations, independently of its legal status at the trial (Bass 2000: 302).

In short, through deterrence and collective memory functions, criminal trials may help transitions and prevent the repetition of past evil. Optimism, however, must be tempered by insights into the selectivity and inaccuracy of trial-based memories, by the focus on "small fish" in the absence of regime transitions and by transition problems that trials may cause in some contexts.

What is the role of alternative responses to human rights violations?

Fortunately, criminal courts are not facing the task alone. A balance of principles may be more realistically achieved through a mix of institutions. I select three alternative and supplemental mechanisms out of a great variety that includes UN Treaty bodies, creative new models, truth commission, reparation programs, vetting proceedings, apologies, commemorations and memorials, or amnesties.

Treaty bodies, regional courts and the world court?

While the movement toward criminal justice and other mechanisms has partly been powered by a profound sense of frustration regarding the weak enforcement of HR through UN Treaty bodies and traditional international courts (Sikkink 2009), the latter institutions still constitute one crucial component in the mix of mechanisms through which the international community responds to HR violations.

UN HR bodies include Charter bodies and Treaty bodies in the narrow sense of the term (for formal descriptions and details see the web site of the Office of the High Commissioner for Human Rights: http://www.ohchr.org/EN/Pages/WelcomePage.aspx). Charter bodies prominently include the Security Council, the General Assembly, and the Human Rights Council (HRC). The HRC meets in Geneva ten weeks a year and comprises 47 elected member states of the UN. Its purpose is the prevention of HR abuses. Treaty bodies in the narrow sense of the term include the:

- Human Rights Committee

- Committee on Economic, Social and Cultural Rights

- Committee on the Elimination of Racial Discrimination

- Committee on the Elimination of Discrimination Against Women

- Committee on the Rights of the Child

- Committee Against Torture & Optional Protocol to the Convention against Torture—Subcommittee on Prevention of Torture

These committees of independent experts are charged to monitor the implementation of core international HR treaties. They can find states to be in contempt of HR conventions, and they can suggest remedies. Yet, their enforcement powers are extremely limited.

International courts beyond the criminal courts discussed above include the International Court of Justice (ICJ), also called the "world court," and regional courts. These are not criminal courts. In fact, individuals do not have legal standing in this ICJ. Instead, the court addresses disputes between states, and it provides the UN with advisory opinions. Regional courts such as the European Court of Human Rights (ECHR) and the Inter-American Court of Human Rights have somewhat stronger enforcement mechanisms. Also, here individuals have legal standing. Citizens of European countries, for example, could file grievances regarding the infringement of their HR with the ECHR. The court would test these grievances against The European Convention for the Protection of Human Rights and Fundamental Freedoms. Its judgments may demand reparation and force policy changes in member countries. Judgments also become binding law to nation-level courts.

From modern criminal justice back into the future?— Gacacas in Rwanda

Post-genocidal Rwanda provides an illustration for how alternative institutions may be created that draw on models of traditional justice (Meyerstein 2007). It also shows how such institutions can co-exist with domestic and international criminal court proceedings. Both respond to the Rwandan genocide of 1994, during which some 800,000 people, mostly of the Tutsi population were killed, tens of thousands of women raped, and innumerous victims tortured and mutilated in one of the most intense killing episodes of the twentieth century.

The new institution was called *inkiko gacaca* (*gacaca*). The word is derived from the local Kinyarwandan language and refers to the lawn where disputes among neighbors were traditionally arbitrated. The *gacaca*, while inspired by traditional justice forms, is a modern system of some 10,000 community-based judicial bodies, oriented toward retributive and restorative justice, and administered by the Rwandan state. By establishing the *gacaca*, the state responded to a desperate situation in which up to 120,000 detainees waited for their trials in overcrowded cells in this extremely poor country of just six million people. It was calculated that it would take more than half a century to process all genocide-related cases through the decimated regular court system (Meyerstein 2007: 473).

Each *gacaca* consists of a General Assembly, made up of all adult inhabitants of the smallest administrative units of the state, and a Bench with nine judges (there are over 100,000 judges in total). Decisions by local *gacacas* can be appealed at higher level *gacaca* courts. The goal of the *gacacas* was five-fold: to reveal truth, to accelerate trials, to end impunity, to achieve a sense of reconciliation and to document Rwanda's ability to manage the situation independently. The *gacacas* had jurisdiction over cases of murder or attempted murder and property crimes, where the maximum penalty is 30 years in prison (offense categories 1 and 2). Only criminal courts had jurisdiction over category 1 perpetrators, "planners, organizers, inciters, supervisors and ringleaders of the genocide" (Organic Law 2004, quoted after Meyerstein 2007: 474).

Gacaca Bench deliberations are confidential, but decisions are made public. Benches have the authority to summon people to testify, to issue search warrants, impose criminal sanctions and confiscate property. Proceedings entail three phases; during the pretrial phase General Assemblies collect information on the victims, property damage and suspected perpetrators. Benches then meet confidentially to assess the testimony and assign suspects to perpetrator categories (in 2006, some 70,000 accused were placed in category 1, some 400,000 in category 2 and some 300,000 in category 3). Finally, the judgment phase is held in the appropriate courts.

The *gacacas* have been severely criticized by human rights organizations such as Amnesty International (AI) for going against several principles laid down in the UDHR, especially Article 14(1) of the International Covenant on Civil and Political Rights that demands "Equality of Arms" in criminal courts, the defendants' right to defense council of their choice. Further critics address vague language of the law that endangers impartiality and the lack of judicial competence that results from the brevity of *gacaca*-judges' legal training. Responding to such critique, the Rwanda Supreme Court and other NGOs such as Penal Reform International (PRI) have stressed the practical constraints faced by the Rwandan justice system, and the tension between Western trial standards and the right to a speedy trial. Applying a "weak form of cultural relativism," they argue, for example, that the absence of defense council is compensated for by the mass participatory nature of the proceedings that assures proper fact finding (Meyerstein 2007: 481). The Rwandan Supreme Court considers it difficult to "condemn unjustly an innocent in front of the entire population of the cell [the smallest administrative unit], who have the same information as the accuser and when everyone has the right to express their opinion freely" (quoted after Meyerstein 2007: 481).

What is at stake here, according to Meyerstein, is the emergence of a new vision of HR, going beyond the dichotomy of strict adherence to a Western model of justice versus the restorative and conciliatory approach of truth commissions Teitel (2000) distinguishes in her famous discussion of transitional justice regimes. Instead,

> the *gacaca* both accept and resist the dominant international legalist model but do so from a standpoint of culture, rather than sovereignty. Moreover this particularized form is attentive to the needs of postcolonial society in the developing world and in its emphasis on communal development and reconstruction driven by local, informal processes (Meyerstein 2007: 492).

Meyerstein's is a plea for legal pluralism and an optimistic assessment of its potential. It invites different forms of achieving justice, combined with truth seeking and restorative agendas, that are sensitive to the political, cultural, and economic context of transitional "third world" societies. This dissent between strict proponents of universalistic models of rights versus legal pluralists thus constitutes one additional field of tension in the world of HR law.

Truth commissions as alternatives or supplements?

Truth commissions (TC) are bodies that focus on the past, investigate long-lasting patterns of abuses, are constituted for limited periods of time and conclude their work with a report. They are officially sanctioned and authorized by the state. This definition underlies the most profound comparative study of 21 truth commissions to date, including those of Argentina, Chile, El Salvador, Guatemala, Germany, Uganda, and South Africa (Hayner 2001). Most TCs share additional characteristics in that they focus on the recent past, were established during a political transition, and investigate politically motivated repression.

Most also have the same set of basic goals, even if the focus will vary: to bring to light and officially acknowledge past abuses, to respond to victims' needs, to set the stage for justice and accountability, to recommend institutional changes, and to promote reconciliation (Hayner 2001: 24). The name "TC" is often misleading as the truth is frequently well known, while its acknowledgement is at stake.

The Argentinean TC, for example, the National Commission on the Disappeared was created in 1983 per decree by President Raúl Alfonsín after seven years of military dictatorship, during which tens of thousands endured arrest and torture and "were disappeared." Alfonsin appointed ten commissioners, representing different sectors of society, some of whom had a track record of HR advocacy. Most HR organizations supported the commission and turned over scores of information on the disappeared. Yet, the Armed Forces refused to cooperate, and the commission had no means to enforce their assistance.

While commission hearings were not held in public, the work nevertheless produced much publicity as exiles returned home to testify and commission staff visited former torture centers and secret cemeteries. Taking over 7,000 statements, including over 1,500 from survivors of detention camps, the commission documented camp conditions, torture practices, lists of 365 former torture centers and of 8,960 disappeared persons. The report the commission delivered after nine months became a best-seller in Argentina. Also, the commission turned its files over to the prosecutor's office and thus provided critical evidence for the cases against senior members of the military Junta.

In South Africa a TC was seriously considered after Nelson Mandela's election to President. In 1995 the legislature passed the Promotion of National Unity and Reconciliation Act, which constituted the 17-member TRC with Bishop Desmond Tutu as chair. The Act armed the commission with considerable authority and investigatory reach (regarding search and seizure, subpoena, and witness protection) and also with the power to grant amnesties to individuals who confessed fully to having committed politically motivated crimes. Three sub-commissions were responsible, respectively, for collecting statements from victims and witnesses of gross HR violations (21,000 were collected by the HR Violations Committee); decide on individual applications for amnesty (Amnesty Committee), and design a reparations program (Reparations and Rehabilitation Committee). The South African model is, at the macro-level, most closely related to criminologist John Braithwaite's (1989) idea of "reintegrative shaming."

Like the Argentinean commission, the TRC also attracted consider-able publicity. Two thousand victims and witnesses appeared in public hearings; special hearings focused on the role of key societal institu-tions; several hours of hearings were broadcast daily on national radio; and a Sunday night TV program on the commission's work became the most-watched news program in the country. Yet, the TRC was critiqued for not making much use of the extensive powers it was given, due to its focus on reconciliation rather than accountability.

The differences between the Argentinean and the South African cases illustrate what a broader review confirms: the relationship between TCs and criminal justice responses to grave HR violations is variable. In El Salvador, the TC report prompted a general amnesty. Like in Argentina, TCs in Uganda and Haiti produced evidence that supported later prose-cutions. In Chile the TC worked under an amnesty law that was already in place; but its work later strengthened international prosecutions. Only in South Africa was the TRC authorized to offer amnesties to spe-cific perpetrators (for details see Hayner 2001: 90). Supporters argue that TCs are not accompanied or followed by trials only in those cases where economic constraints, lack of training, corrupt "justice" systems, or the continuing influence of past perpetrators offers little hope for effective prosecution in the first place.

Finally, TCs may contribute to accountability in ways not available to criminal courts. For example, instead of attributing responsibility to particular individuals alone, they may examine broader patterns of abuse, thereby encouraging institutional reforms. They may thus also challenge broad sectors of society and segments of the population that carry some degree of responsibility, from bureaucrats to torturers and profiteers all the way to by-standers who refused to speak up. Yet, the work of TRCs faces limits as well, even in their contribution to the con-struction of history. Critics stress that TRCs are more concerned with col-lective well-being than with the fate of individuals. Wilson (2001) cites Plato, for whom the interest of the state is the ultimate standard, and he places reconciliation proponents such as legal scholar Martha Minow (1998, 2002) and activist Desmond Tutu in this tradition. Especially where old power holders maintain positions of authority (e.g., Pinochet in Chile, de Klerk in South Africa), he argues, amnesties are seen as a necessary political compromise, at times paired with TRCs. He concludes in resignation: "A culture of human rights was constructed upon the quicksand of a culture of impunity" (Wilson 2003: 369).

Not surprising then, the overall record of TCs is mixed. Their functioning is contingent on the competitive games between various actors who control diverse types of material or symbolic capital, just like in the case of the ICTY illustrated above. Some commissions overcame neither massive barriers in their search for evidence nor pressure from power-holders. Some did not succeed to attract much publicity. Commissions in Bolivia and Ecuador did not complete their work. Those in Burundi and Zimbabwe produced reports that were never made public. Not surprisingly, like the unsuccessful TC of Uganda, the latter two did not unfold in the context of fundamental regime change.

In short, the institution of TCs is new, one of many attempts begun in the twentieth century to address gross HR violations. Importantly, they must not be regarded in isolation, but in the context of other institutions, some of which they may in fact strengthen, including criminal justice responses.

A new era?

Criminal courts (domestic, foreign, international, or hybrid), newly created justice mechanisms such as *gacacas*, truth commissions of various sorts, UN Treaty bodies and international, mostly regional, HR courts are only some of the institutional mechanisms developed in the course of the second half of the twentieth century. They are joined by others. Lustration (or vetting) proceedings bar entire groups of people who had been involved in past regimes with grave HR violations from occupying public office in post-transition eras (*Law and Social Inquiry* 1995). Amnesties that acknowledge past violations but offer perpetrators impunity often play a central role in transitions (Mallinder 2008). Finally, the number of apologies by state leaders for recent and long-past atrocities has increased exponentially (Bilder 2008). Much as these mechanisms differ from each other, they all confirm Minow's (2002) diagnosis that, while many centuries can compete with the twentieth for the massive abuses against humans by governments, it is distinct in that it gave rise to a movement of innovative institutional responses.

We have discussed why responses to human rights violations have become more likely and more punitive in modernity. We saw that diverse mechanisms can coexist and cooperate, depending on social context. We have raised questions about the chances that they will indeed reduce gross HL and HR violations, and we have provided some preliminary answers. Hope is guarded with caution. Today massive killing and rape campaigns are underway in the Democratic Republic of Congo and are continuing in Darfur. Intense repression is practiced in Zimbabwe and Myanmar. The freedom of press is severely constrained in Russia. The United States is just coming out of the Iraq war that was at least problematic in terms of international law, and it faces charges of torture and illegal confinement. The PRC did not even allow small protests by members of civil society during the 2008 Olympic Games in Beijing, and access to free information is systematically restrained. In Pakistan the government looks on as young women are being buried alive because they do not consent to arranged marriages. In Cambodia and elsewhere young girls are forced into prostitution. In Europe, Sinti and Roma continue to experience massive discrimination. A complete list would fill another volume.

Our brief journey through a large terrain is coming to its end. We have learned that the struggle for the protection of HR through multiple innovative mechanisms, including international criminal justice institutions, is in full force. We also recognize that participants in this struggle face difficult dilemmas and are up against massive impediments and mighty opponents. Believing neither in the absolute sanctity of the principle of state sovereignty, nor in military intervention as an optimal solution, many welcome this new inventiveness.

Finally, on the side of scholarship and for the sake of more effective remedies, I hope to have shown that mainstream criminologists must begin to place the issue of humanitarian and HR crimes high on their agenda and learn from other fields. Simultaneously HR scholars should avail themselves of criminological insights. There is no time to lose.

References

Alexander, Jeffrey C. et al. 2004. *Cultural Trauma and Collective Identity*. Berkeley: University of California Press.

Anderson, Elijah. 1994. *Code of the Street*. New York: W.W. Norton.

Archer, Dane, and Rosemary Gartner. 1984. *Violence and Crime in Cross-National Perspective*. New Haven: Yale University Press.

Arendt, Hannah. 1964. *Eichmann in Jerusalem: A Report on the Banality of Evil*. New York: Viking Press, 2nd edition.

Bass, Gary J. 2000. *Stay the Hand of Vengeance: The Politics of War Crimes Tribunals*. Princeton: Princeton University Press.

Bauman, Zygmunt. 1989. *Modernity and the Holocaust*. Ithaca: New York University Press.

Becker, Howard S. 1963. *The Other Side*. Glencoe: Free Press.

Bendix, Reinhard. 1996. *Nation-building and Citizenship*. New Brunswick: Transaction Publishers, enlarged edition.

Benford, Robert D., and David A. Snow. 2000. "Framing Processes and Social Movements." *Annual Review of Sociology* 26: 611–39.

Bilder, Richard B. 2006. "The Role of Apology in International Law and Diplomacy." *Virginia Journal of International Law* 46(3): 433–73.

Blau, Judith, and Alberto Moncada. 2007. "'It Ought to be a Crime': Criminalizing Human Rights Violations." *Sociological Forum* 22(3): 364–71.

Borneman, John. 1997. *Settling Accounts: Violence, Justice, and Accountability in Postsocialist Europe*. Princeton: Princeton University Press.

Bourdieu, Pierre. 1987. "The Force of Law: Toward a Sociology of the Judicial Field." *Hastings Law Journal* 38: 805–53.

Boyle, Elizabeth Heger. 2003. *Female Genital Cutting*. Baltimore: Johns Hopkins University Press.

Braithwaite, John. 1989. *Crime, Shame and Reintegration*. Cambridge: Cambridge University Press.

Brannigen, A., and K.H. Hardwick. 2003. "Genocide and General Theory." Pp. 109–31 in C. Britt and M.R. Gottfredson, eds. *Control Theories in Crime and Delinquency*. New Brunswick: Transaction Publishers.

Browning, Christopher R. 1998. *Ordinary Men: Police Battalion 101 and the Final Solution in Poland*. New York: Harper Collins, 2nd edition.

Brustein, William. 1996. *The Logic of Evil*. New Haven: Yale University Press.

Cerulo, Karen A. 2007. "The Forum Mailbag." *Sociological Forum* 22(4): 555–65

Chambliss, William J. 1989. "State Organized Crime." *Criminology* 27: 183–208.

Chang, Jung, and Jon Halliday. 2005. *Mao: The Unknown Story.* London: Cape.

Coffee, John C. 1981. "'No Soul to Damn, no Body to Kick.' An Unscandalized Inquiry into the Problem of Corporate Punishment." *Michigan Law Review* 79: 386–459.

Cohen, Albert K. 1955. *Delinquent Boys*. Glencoe: Free Press.

Cohen, Lawrence E., and Marcus Felson.1979. "Social Change and Crime Rate Trends: A Routine Activity Approach." *American Sociological Review* 44: 588–608.

Cohen, Stanley. 2001. *States of Denial: Knowing about Atrocities and Suffering.* Cambridge: Polity Press.

Cole, Wade M. 2005. "Sovereignty Relinquished? Explaining Commitment to the International Human Rights Covenants, 1966–1999." *American Sociological Review* 70(3): 472–95.

Coleman, James. 2006. *The Criminal Elite*. New York: Worth.

Coleman, James S. 1990. *Foundations of Social Theory*. Cambridge: The Belknap Press of Harvard University Press.

Collins, Randall. 2008. *Violence*. Princeton: Princeton University Press.

Cooney, Mark. 1997. "From Warre to Tyranny: Lethal Conflict and the State." *American Sociological Review* 62: 316–38.

Dimsdale, Joel E. ed. 1980. *Survivors, Victims, and Perpetrators*. Washington: Hemisphere.

Durkheim, Emile. 1961. *Moral Education*. Glencoe: Free Press.

_____. [1912] 2001. *The Elementary Forms of Religious Life*. Oxford: Oxford University Press.

Eisner, Manuel. 2001. "Modernization, Self-control and Lethal Violence." *British Journal of Criminology* 41(4): 618–38.

Elias, Norbert. 1978. *The Civilizing Process*. New York: Urizen.

Ermann, M. David and Richard J. Lundman eds. 2002. *Corporate and Governmental Deviance.* Oxford: Oxford University Press.

Etzioni, Amitai. 1993. "The US Sentencing Commission on Corporate Crime: A Critique." *The Annals of the American Academy of Political and Social Science* 525: 147–56.

Fein, Helen. 1979. *Accounting for Genocide*. Chicago: University of Chicago Press.

Feldman, Noah. 2008. "When Judges Make Foreign Policy." *The New York Times Magazine*, September 28, pp. 50–57, 66, 70.

Fichtelberg, Aaron. 2005. "Crimes Beyond Justice? Retributivism and War Crimes Trials." *Criminal Justice Ethics* 24(2): 31–46.

_____. 2008. *Crime Without Borders*. Upper Saddle River, NJ: Pearson.

Foucault, Michel. 1975. *Discipline and Punish*. London: Penguin.

Friedländer, Saul. 2007. *The Years of Extermination. Nazi Germany and the Jews, 1939–1945*. New York: Harper.

Garfinkel, Harold. 1956. "Conditions of Successful Degradation Ceremonies." *American Journal of Sociology* 61: 420–24.

Garland, David. 1990. *Punishment in Modern Society*. Chicago: University of Chicago Press.

_____. 2001. *The Culture of Control*. Chicago: University of Chicago Press.

Giesen, Bernhard. 2004. *Triumph or Trauma*. Boulder: Paradigm.

Giordano, Peggy C., Stephen A. Cernkovich, and Jennifer L. Rudolph. 2002. "Gender, Crime, and Desistance: Toward a Theory of Cognitive Transformation." *American Journal of Sociology* 107: 990–1064.

Goldhagen, Daniel J. 1996. *Hitler's Willing Executioners: Ordinary Germans and the Holocaust*. New York: Alfred A. Knopf.

Goldsmith, Jack, and Stephen D. Krasner. 2003. "The Limits of Idealism." *Daedalus* 132(47): 47–63.

Goldstein, Joseph, Burke Marshall, and Jack Schwartz. 1976. *The My Lai Massacre and its Cover-up: Beyond the Reach of Law? The Peers Commission Report with a Supplement and an Introductory Essay on the Limits of Law*. New York: Free Press.

Hagan, John. 2003. *Justice in the Balkans*. Chicago: University of Chicago Press.

Hagan, John, and Ron Levi. 2005. "Crimes of War and the Force of Law." *Social Forces* 83(4): 1499–534.

_____. 2007. "Justiciability as Field Effect: When Sociology Meets Human Rights." *Sociological Forum* 22(3): 372–84.

Hagan, John, and Wenona Rymond-Richmond. 2009. *Darfur and the Crime of Genocide*. Cambridge: Cambridge University Press.

Halbwachs, Maurice. 1992. *On Collective Memory*. Chicago: University of Chicago Press.

Hayner, Priscilla B. 2001. *Unspeakable Truths: Confronting State Terror and Atrocities*. New York: Routledge.

Heberer, Patricia, and Jürgen Matthäus, eds. 2008. *Atrocities on Trial*. Lincoln: University of Nebraska Press.

Hersh, Seymour M. 1970. *My Lai 4*. New York: Random House.

Hilberg, Raul. [1961] 2003. *The Destruction of the European Jews*. New Haven: Yale University Press.

Hirschi, Travis. 1969. *Causes of Delinquency*. Berkeley: University of California Press.

Horowitz, Louis Irving. 2002. *Tanking Lives: Genocide and State Power*. New Brunswick: Transaction Publishers, 5th edition.

Hughes, Everett. 1963. "Good People and Dirty Work." Pp. 23–36 in Howard Becker, ed. *The Other Side*. New York: Free Press.

Jensen, Gary. 2007. *The Path of the Devil: Early Modern Witch Hunts*. Lanham: Rowman & Littlefield.

Johnson, Eric A., and Eric H. Monkkonen, eds. 1996. *The Civilization of Crime*. Urbana: University of Illinois Press.

Joods Historisch Museum Amsterdam. 1969. *Documents of the Persecution of the Dutch Jewry 1940–1945*. Amsterdam: Polak & Van Gennep.

Katz, Jack. 1988. *Seductions of Crime*. New York: Basic Books.

Keck, Margaret E., and Kathryn Sikkink. 1998. *Activists without Borders*. Ithaca: Cornell.

Keegan, John. 1976. *The Face of Battle*. London: Cape.

Khan, Mahvish Rukhsana. 2008. *My Guantánamo Diary*. New York: Public Affairs.

Kramer, Ronald, and Raymond Michalowski. 2005. "War, Aggression and State Crime: A Criminological Analysis of the Invasion and Occupation of Iraq." *British Journal of Criminology* 45(4): 446–69.

Landsman, Stephen. 2005. *Crimes of the Holocaust: The Law Confronts Hard Cases*. Philadelphia: University of Pennsylvania Press.

Law and Social Inquiry, Vol. 20, No. 1, 1995 (special issue on lustration).

Levi, Primo. 1989. *The Drowned and the Saved*. New York: Vintage.

Lofquist, William S. 1993. "Organizational Probation and the US Sentencing Commission." *The Annals of the American Academy of Political and Social Science* 525: 157–69.

Mallinder, Louise. 2008. *Amnesties, Human Rights and Political Transitions*. Oxford: Hart.

Manza, Jeff, and Christopher Uggen. 2006. *Locked Out: Felon Disenfranchisement and American Democracy*. New York: Oxford University Press.

Matsueda, Ross L. 2006. "Differential Social Organization, Collective Action, and Crime." *Crime, Law and Social Change* 46(1–2): 3–33.

Matsueda, Ross L., Derek A. Kreager, and David Huizinga. 2006. "Deterring Delinquents: A Rational Choice Model of Theft and Violence." *American Sociological Review* 71(1): 95–122.

Meierhenrich, Jens. 2006. "Conspiracy in International Law." *Annual Review of Law and Social Science* 2: 341–57.

Mental Health Advisory Team (MHAT). 2006. IV–Operation Iraqi Freedom 05–07. 2006. Final Report of November 17, 2006. Office of the Surgeon, Multi-national Force-Iraq, and Office of the Surgeon General, United States Army Medical Command.

Merton, Robert K. 1938. "Social Structure and Anomie." *American Sociological Review* 3: 672–82.

Messner, Steven F., and Richard Rosenfeld. 2007. *Crime and the American Dream*. Belmont: Wadsworth, 4th edition.

Meyer, John, John Boli, George Thomas, and Francisco Ramirez. 1997. "World Society and the Nation State." *American Journal of Sociology* 103(1): 144–81.

Meyerstein, Ariel. 2007. "Between Law and Culture: Rwanda's *Gacaca* and Postcolonial Legality." *Law and Social Inquiry* 32(2): 467–508.

Milgram, Stanley. 1965. "Some Conditions of Obedience and Disobedience to Authority." *Human Relations* 18(1): 57–75.

Minow, Martha. 1998. *Between Vengeance and Forgiveness: Facing History after Genocide and Mass Violence.* Boston:Beacon Press.

_____. 2002. *Breaking the Cycles of Hatred: Memory, Law, and Repair, Introduced and with Commentaries by NL Rosenblum.* Princeton: Princeton University Press.

Neurath, Paul Martin. [1943] 2005. *The Society of Terror: Inside the Dachau and Buchenwald Concentration Camps.* London: Paradigm.

Nino, Carlos S. 1996. *Radical Evil on Trial.* New Haven: Yale University Press.

Nunca Mas. 1986. *Report by Argentina's National Commission on Disappeared People.* London: Farber and Farber.

Orwell, George. 1949. *Nineteen Eighty-four.* New York: Harcourt, Brace.

Osiel, Mark J. 1997. *Mass Atrocities, Collective Memory, and the Law.* New Brunswick: Transaction Publishers.

Pensky, Max. 2008. "Amnesty on Trial: Impunity, Accountability, and the Norms of International Law." *Ethics & Global Politics* 1(1–2): 1–40.

Power, Samantha. 2002. *A Problem from Hell: America and the Age of Genocide.* New York: Harper.

Rafter, Nicole. 1988. *White Trash: The Eugenic Family Studies, 1877–1919.* Boston: Northeastern University Press.

Rosen, David M. 2007. "Child Soldiers, International Humanitarian Law, and the Globalization of Childhood." *American Anthropologist* 109(2): 296–306.

Roht-Arriaza, Naomi. 2005. *The Pinochet Effect: Transnational Justice in the Age of Human Rights.* Philadelphia: University of Pennsylvania Press.

Rummel, R.J. 1994. *Death by Government.* New Brunswick: Transaction Publishers.

Rusche, Georg, and Otto Kirchheimer. 2003. *Punishment and Social Structure,* with a new Introduction by Dario Melossi. New Brunswick: Transaction Publishers.

Sampson, Robert J., and John H. Laub. 1993. *Crime in the Making.* Cambridge: Harvard University Press.

Sampson, Robert J., and Stephen W. Raudenbush. 1999. "Systematic Social Observation of Public Spaces: A New Look at Disorder in Urban Neighborhoods." *American Journal of Sociology* 105: 603–51.

Savelsberg, Joachim J. 1992. "Law That Does Not Fit Society: Sentencing Guidelines as a Neo-classical Reaction to the Dilemmas of Substantivized Law." *American Journal of Sociology* 97: 1346–81.

_____. 1994. "Knowledge, Domination, and Criminal Punishment." *American Journal of Sociology* 99: 911–43.

_____. 1999. "Knowledge, Domination, and Criminal Punishment Revisited: Incorporating State Socialism." *Punishment and Society* 1(1): 45–70.

Savelsberg, Joachim J., with Peter Brühl. 1994. *Constructing White-collar Crime*. Philadelphia: University of Pennsylvania Press.

Savelsberg Joachim J., and Ryan D. King. 2007. "Law and Collective Memory." *Annual Review of Law and Social Science* 3: 189–211.

_____. 2010. *Atrocities, Law and Collective Memory*. New York: Russell Sage.

Schabas, William A. 2007. *An Introduction to the International Criminal Court*. Cambridge: Cambridge University Press.

Schrager, Laura Shill, and James F. Short. 1980. "How Serious a Crime: Perceptions of Organizational and Common Crimes." Pp. 14–31 in Gilbert Geis and Ezra Stotland, eds. *White-collar Crime*. Beverly Hills: Sage.

Sikkink, Kathryn. 2009. "From State Responsibility to Individual Criminal Accountability: A New Regulatory Model for Core Human Rights Violations." Pp. 121–150 in Walter Mattli and Ngaire Woods, eds. *The Politics of Global Regulation*. Princeton: Princeton University Press.

Sikkink, Kathryn, and Carrie Booth-Walling. 2007. "The Impact of Human Rights Trials in Latin America." *Journal of Peace Research* 44(4): 427–45.

Sikkink, Kathryn, and Hunjoon Kim. 2010. "Explaining the Deterrence Effect of Human Rights Prosecutions in Transitional Countries." *International Studies Quarterly*.

Simmel, Georg. [1908] 1968. *Soziologie*. Berlin: Duncker und Humblot.

Simon, Jonathan. 2007. *Governing Through Crime*. Oxford: Oxford University Press.

Smith, Philip. 2008. Punishment and Culture. Chicago: University of Chicago Press.

Snyder, Jack, and Leslie Vinjamuri. 2003/2004. "Trials and Errors: Principle and Pragmatism in Strategies of International Justice." *International Security* 28: 5–44.

Sofsky, Wolfgang. 1996. *The Order of Terror: The Concentration Camp*. Princeton: Princeton University Press.

Steinmetz, George. 2007. *The Devil's Handwriting: Precoloniality and the German Colonial State in Qingdao, Samoa, and Southwest Africa*. Chicago: University of Chicago Press.

Stewart, James G. 2006. "Rethinking Guantánamo: Unlawful Confinement as Applied in International Criminal Law." *Journal of International Criminal Justice* 4: 12–30.

Stolleis, Michael. 2007. "Law and Lawyers Preparing the Holocaust." *Annual Review of Law and Social Science* 3: 213–32.

Stouffer, Samuel Andrew, et al. 1949. *The American Soldier*. Princeton: Princeton University Press.

Stover, Eric. 2005. *The Witnesses: War Crimes and the Promise of Justice in The Hague*. Philadelphia: University of Pennsylvania Press.

Sutherland, Edwin H. 1940. "White Collar Criminality." *American Sociological Review* 5: 1–12.

_____. 1983. *White Collar Crime: The Uncut Version*, with an Introduction by Gilbert Geis and Collin Goff. New Haven: Yale University Press.

Sutherland, Edwin H., and Donald R. Cressey. 1974. *Criminology*. Philadelphia: J.B. Lippincott, 9th edition.

Sutton, John R. 2000. "Imprisonment and Social Classification in five Common-law Democracies, 1955–1985." *American Journal of Sociology* 106: 350–85.

Sykes, Grasham M., and David Matza. 1957. "Techniques of Neutralization: A Theory of Delinquency." *American Sociological Review* 22: 664–70.

Teitel, Ruti G. 2000. *Transitional Justice*. Oxford: Oxford University Press.

Thompson, E.P. 1975. *Whigs and Hunters*. New York: Pantheon.

Tittle, Charles R. 1995. *Control Balance*. Boulder: Westview Press.

Todorov, Tzvetan. 1995. "Communist Camps and their Aftermath." *Representations* 49: 120–32.

Turk, Austin. 1982. *Political Criminology*. Thousand Oaks: Sage.

Vaughan, Diane. 1999. "The Dark Side of Organizations: Mistake, Misconduct, and Disaster." *Annual Review of Sociology* 25: 271–305.

_____. 2002. "Criminology and the Sociology of Organizations." *Crime, Law, and Social Change* 37: 117–36.

Waller, James. 2007. *Becoming Evil*. Oxford: Oxford University Press.

Weber, Max. 1976. *Economy and Society*. Berkeley: University of California Press.

Weitz, Eric D. 2003. *A Century of Genocide: Utopias of Race and Nation*. Princeton: Princeton University Press.

Wheeler, Stanton, and Mitchell L. Rothman. 1982. "The Organization as a Weapon in White Collar Crime." *Michigan Law Review* 80: 1403–26.

William, Archbishop of Tyre. 1943. *A History of Deeds Done Beyond the Sea*, translated and annotated by Emily Atwater Babcock and A.C. Krey. New York: Columbia University Press.

Wilson, Richard A. 2001. *The Politics of the Truth and Reconciliation Commission in South Africa*. Cambridge: Cambridge University Press.

_____. 2003. "Anthropological Studies of National Reconciliation Processes." *Anthropological Theory* 3: 367–87.

Wolfgang, Marvin E., and Franco Feracuti. 1982. *The Subculture of Violence*. Beverly Hills: Sage.

Zimbardo, Philip. 2007. *The Lucifer Effect: Understanding How Good People Turn Evil*. New York: Random House.

Zimmerer, Jürgen. 2005. "The Birth of the Ostland out of the Spirit of Colonialism: a Postcolonial Perspective of the Nazi Policy of Conquest and Extermination." *Patterns of Prejudice* 39(2): 197–219.

Index

Page references in **bold** indicate tables, those in *italic* indicate maps.

Available in the Compact Criminology series.

crime and human rights
Joachim J. Savelsberg

crime and risk
Pat O'Malley

comparative criminal justice
David Nelken

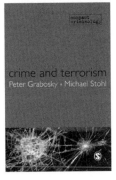

crime and terrorism
Peter Grabosky • Michael Stohl

experimental criminology
Lawrence Sherman

compact
criminology